D1538390

Information Literacy and the School Library Media Center

DISCARDED

Recent titles in Greenwood Professional Guides in School Librarianship

Harriet Selverstone, Series Editor

Information Literacy and the School Library Media Center

Joie Taylor

028.7071
TAY

YPX322914

Libraries Unlimited Professional Guides
in School Librarianship

Harriet Selverstone, Series Editor

LIBRARIES

U N L I M I T E D

A Member of the Greenwood Publishing Group

Westport, Connecticut ● London

Library of Congress Cataloging-in-Publication Data

Taylor, Joie.
  Information literacy and the school library media center / by Joie Taylor.
    p. cm. — (Libraries Unlimited professional guides in school librarianship)
  ISBN 0-313-32020-9 (pbk. : alk. paper)
    1. Information literacy—Study and teaching—United States. 2. Information literacy—
  Standards—United States. 3. School libraries—Activity programs—United States. 4. School
  librarian participation in curriculum planning—United States. I. Title. II. Series.
  ZA3075.T39   2005
  028.7071—dc22   2005026148

British Library Cataloguing in Publication Data is available.

Copyright © 2006 by Joie Taylor

All rights reserved. No portion of this book may be
reproduced, by any process or technique, without the
express written consent of the publisher.

Library of Congress Catalog Card Number: 2005026148
ISBN: 0-313-32020-9

First published in 2006

Libraries Unlimited, 88 Post Road West, Westport, CT 06881
A Member of the Greenwood Publishing Group, Inc.
www.lu.com

Printed in the United States of America

The paper used in this book complies with the
Permanent Paper Standard issued by the National
Information Standards Organization (Z39.48–1984).

10   9   8   7   6   5   4   3

Contents

List of Figures

Acknowledgments

I would be remiss if I did not give special thanks to Harriet Silverstone, who read the manuscript and made valuable suggestions, and to Sharon Coatney for her patience as I worked through this project. I would not have made it this far without their help, support, and understanding.

Introduction

In the one-room school I attended for grades K–5, we had a small room we called the library. There were four shelves from which the teacher told me I could take books to read. In the six years I attended the school, I never did find out who used the other books. I don't remember ever getting new ones. We did not do any research, as all the information we needed was in our textbooks. I learned about card catalogs and author, title, and subject cards, not because we had a card catalog (which we didn't), but because those questions were on the Iowa Tests of Basic Skills. I discovered once I got to high school that just because I could answer the test questions didn't mean I could use the library.

My schooling began more than 50 years ago. Much has changed since then, including our information needs. The local neighborhood and the nearby town defined my world. As a result my information needs were few and readily available from my parents or the newspaper. The same cannot be said for children today. Their world is full of news from strange-sounding places like Uzbekistan, and they hear about poverty and war in Sudan. Many have physically traveled to different parts of the United States or made virtual trips via the Internet and television to other parts of the world. I grew up in a homogeneous community, but students today have in their classrooms children from various cultures, some of whom do not speak English. To say that children today have greater information needs and need access to more information is something of an understatement.

The amount of information keeps increasing; therefore students must become discerning consumers of information. As a K–12 student I could be assured that the books I used had been edited, the information was accurate, and the author was someone who knew the subject. Not so today! Anyone can publish on the Internet. One needs no special training, no specific knowledge in a subject area, and no editor. Consequently much of what is published on the Internet is suspect. The information must be scrutinized for accuracy, authority, and bias. These are skills that students must learn. In other words, students must become critical thinkers. An information literacy curriculum provides the standards for students to become critical users of information.

The library media specialist is the person responsible for teaching the information literacy curriculum in many schools. Since becoming information literate is an active process, one in which the learner must actively seek knowledge rather than just sitting and absorbing facts, a different type of teaching methodology must evolve. The library media specialist must become a coach guiding the students through a research process.

Teaching a research process is an important part of becoming information literate. A person's need for information never ends; the type of information needed changes. The reason for the information changes, but the need for information does not. Because of the continuing need for information, knowing a research process is critical. Students must be more self-directed in their learning, and a research process gives them the direction.

Another necessary change to help students in learning information literacy skills is to integrate those skills with what is being done in the classroom. Integration helps them see the relevance of learning the process. Since the learning is tied to something they already know, the students will be more successful.

The integration of information literacy skills with other curricula will require flexible scheduling. No longer can students come to the library media center every Tuesday at 9:00 A.M. for some instruction. With integration the students come when there is a need. If the skills are tied to another curriculum area, coming to the library means coming at the time the class meets and coming for several days in a row.

Because of the integration with other curricula and the increased use of the library media center, the library media specialist will have to consider the use of curriculum mapping and collection mapping. The former helps determine where the skills can be taught. The latter identifies areas of weakness and strengths in the library media collection. Both are needed if the library media center is to serve student's and teacher's needs.

Everyone has information needs—which movie to see, what car to buy, what polymyogia rhumematica is. Information is a fundamental need people have. The school library media specialist today has an important task, that of instructing students to become critical consumers of information. In 1998 the American Association of School Librarians and the Association for Educational Communications and Technology published *Information Power: Building Partnerships for Learning,* which provided national information literacy standards for the first time.

What is information literacy? Why are information literacy skills so important? What are the national standards? How have different states adapted the national standards to meet state standards? What is collaboration and flexible scheduling? How does a library media specialist work with classroom teachers to integrate information literacy skills into other curricular areas? What does the teaching of information literacy look like at the local level? What implications does the teaching of information literacy skills have for the library media center? What research processes are there? These are the questions that I attempt to answer in this book. This is not an exhaustive discussion of the issues, but a beginning. Each person must take what he or she needs and apply it to a local situation.

   Information literacy is at the very foundation of our country. Our Founding Fathers were well read, read several languages, and when faced with establishing a government, drew on what information they had, thought about it, and applied the information to the problem. Everyone uses information today regardless of occupation, education, or social and economic status. Educating students to achieve information literacy competence is a goal that must become the heart of the library media program, if not the school. All students need information literacy skills. To neglect teaching students these skills only widens the gap between the haves and the have nots.

CHAPTER 1

Information Literacy: What and Why

A superintendent was explaining to the school board why it was important to continue to support replacing computers in the schools. He commented that the students needed to become information literate. That in the 21st century students needed to know how to use computers to find information. The school district needed to provide computers so students could become information literate.

What is wrong with this picture?

The amount of information available today is increasing rapidly. Information doubles in months rather than years or decades. The widespread use of the Internet has increased access to information to an extent that was unheard of ten years ago. Certainly there is more and more information available to students and teachers, and that information is valuable. Teachers must realize and communicate to students an understanding that in today's society, information is viewed as a commodity and, as such, it is bought and sold, like the product of any other business (Lenox & Walker, 1993, p. 318).

An information glut is here, and undoubtedly information and its availability will continue to increase. This information glut can actually interfere with student learning. The more information students have, the more frustrated they become when trying to understand what they read. To contend with this mass of information, students must have certain skills.

The constructivist philosophy of education contributes to students' need to understand and use information. McKeown and Beck describe constructivism as students constructing their own knowledge and teachers orienting their instructional practices toward teaching for understanding (1999). Constructivism can also be described as inquiry-based learning or problem-solving learning.

1

With all of the information available today and students needing to construct their own meaning, information literacy skills are necessary for them to become functioning, literate adults. What is information literacy? Where did the term originate? Why is it critical? Was the superintendent correct when he equated knowledge of computers with being information literate?

History of Information Literacy

The definition of literacy changes as society's needs change. At one time a person was considered literate if he or she could write his or her name. After the invention of the printing press, to be literate a person had to be able to decode printed words. Today one has to be literate in a variety of ways, one of which is information literacy. Simply decoding words is not enough. The concept of information literacy has been around for about 30 years but has evolved over time. In 1974 Paul Zurkowski, president of the Information Industry Association, introduced the concept of information literacy and defined it as people trained in the application of information resources to their work (cited in Spitzer, Eisenberg & Lowe, 1998). In other words, people use a variety of information tools to mold information solutions to problems. Burchinal stated in 1976 that in order to be information literate people needed a new set of skills, including how to locate and use information efficiently and effectively to solve problems and make decisions (cited in Spitzer, Eisenberg & Lowe, 1998).

Another early definition of information literacy was that it includes all the facts and ideas that one wants at different times for any part of one's life (Carroll, 1981). With this definition Carroll stated the idea that information literacy contains more than needed facts, and she expanded the definition to include the idea that facts could be used in the areas of work, leisure, and personal interest (1981). Here was the suggestion that information could enrich lives.

In response to *A Nation at Risk*, the National Commission on Libraries and Information Science (NCLIS) stated that a basic objective of education is for each student to learn how to identify needed information, locate and organize it, and present it in a clear and persuasive manner (Haskim, 1986, reported in Spitzer, Eisenberg & Lowe, 1998, p. 41). Kuhlthau's work provided the bases for the next stages of development and implementation. She reasoned that existing search processes reflected the information system's perspective rather than the user's perspective. A gap existed between the system's traditional patterns of information provision and the user's natural process of information use (Kuhlthau, 1991). More attention had to be focused on the formative stages of the information search process. More about Kuhlthau's work is reported in Chapter 7.

In 1988 the American Association of School Librarians and the Association for Educational Communications and Technology published *Information Power: Guidelines for School Library Media Programs.* Included was a mission statement that defined the role of the library media program in terms of information needs: The mission of the library media program is to ensure that students and staff are effective users of ideas and information (AASL & AECT, 1988, p. 1). Based on this mission statement, the definition of information literacy as the ability to find and use information was developed (AASL & AECT, 1998). Ten years later *Information Power: Building Partnerships for Learning* stated a set of information standards for student learning. Those standards outline levels of proficiency, provide examples of where information literacy skills might be needed, and offer content-area standards with which information literacy might be integrated (1998).

The International Literacy Year in 1990 ended with *Policy Directions,* which defined literacy as the ability to read and use written information, write appropriately in a range of contexts, and recognize numbers and basic mathematical signs and symbols. The *Policy* also widened the definition to include the integration of speaking, listening, and critical thinking (skills) in reading and writing as well as the idea that literacy develops throughout a person's life (Langford, 1998).

What Is Information Literacy?

Mention the word literacy, and most people will automatically think "reading," but there are a variety of types of literacy that people must have. Among these are reading, visual literacy, computer literacy, numeracy, media literacy, digital literacy, and information literacy. The term *information literacy* can mean different things to different people. Lenox and Walker (1993) define information literacy as a person's ability to access and understand a variety of information sources. Loertscher (1996) says that an information literate student is one who is an avid reader, a critical thinker, a creative thinker, an interested learner, an organized investigator, an effective communicator, a responsible information user, and a skilled user of technology tools.

Another definition of information literacy is the ability to find information, translate it into meaning and understanding, and create good new ideas (McKenzie, 2000). Thompson and Henley (2000) state that information literacy can be defined as knowing how to learn, or the ability to derive meaning from information. Also included in their definition is one from the Association of Supervision and Curriculum Development (ASCD) that defines an information literate student as one who can successfully complete a complex problem-solving process that requires him or her to define the need for information, determine a search strategy, locate the needed resources, assess and understand the information found, interpret the information, communicate the information, and evaluate his or her conclusions in view of the original problem (2000).

Doyle's (1994) definition of information literacy focuses on the attributes of an information literate person. She says that an information literate person is one who

- recognizes that accurate and complete information is the basis for intelligent decision making;

- recognizes the need for information;

- formulates questions based on information needs;

- identifies potential sources of information;

- develops successful search strategies;

- accesses sources of information, including computer-based and other technologies;

- evaluates information;

- organizes information for practical application;

- integrates new information into an existing body of knowledge; and

- uses information in critical thinking and problem solving.

The *Secretary's Commission on Achieving Necessary Skills (SCANS) Report* (2000) indirectly defined information literacy. The report states that a worker who demonstrates competency with information can

- acquire and evaluate information,

- organize and maintain information,

- interpret and communicate information, and

- use computers to process information.

The report suggests that these competencies are needed for the workplace of the future, thus supporting the need for information literacy instruction.

In 1981 the Association of College & Research Libraries, a division of the American Library Association, released its report on information literacy.

It states that to be information literate, a person must be able to recognize when information is needed and have the ability to locate, evaluate, and use effectively the needed information. McKenzie's definition of information literacy has three components:

- Prospecting—requires navigation skills as well as the ability to sort, sift, and select relevant data

- Interpreting—translating data and information into knowledge, insight, and understanding

- Creating good new ideas—development of new ideas rather than rehashing the ideas of others. (2000, pp. 41–42)

The California Technology Assistance Project defines information literacy as a learning process in which one identifies a need or defines a problem, seeks applicable resources, gathers and consumes information, analyzes and interprets the information, synthesizes and effectively communicates the information to others, and evaluates the process (CTAP, 2001).

Many of these definitions have common themes: accessing, locating, evaluating, and using information. Some definitions go further, mentioning the ability to recognize a need for information. In an international study the only component that principals and library media specialists agreed on was the ability to access information from a variety of sources (Oberg, Hay & Henri, 2000). This finding might suggest that educators are still thinking in terms of library skills. Ultimately, information literate people are those who have learned how to learn. They know:

- How knowledge is organized

- How to find information

- How to use information in such a way that others can learn from them. (Radar, 1997, p. 48)

Because there are many definitions for information literacy, school district personnel should agree on a definition for their own use. Defining information literacy is an important first step. All stakeholders (teachers, administrators, and the library media specialist) must understand what is meant by information literacy. Developing a local definition, even if through adaptation of another organization's definition, gives a feeling of ownership to the local educational community. Having agreed on a definition, administrators and teachers must understand the importance of students becoming information literate. They need a process such as Kuhlthau (1994b) developed in order to visualize how students become information literate. Library media specialists must work in collaboration with other teachers and administrators to see that information literacy skills are integrated into all parts of the curricula.

The definition of information literacy used in this book takes a broad view: *the ability to recognize a need, then access, find, evaluate, use, and communicate information.* Learning is the bottom line.

What Information Literacy Is Not

Understanding what information literacy is not is also important. As discussed above, the definition of information literacy has changed over time, and people use different definitions of the term. Say "information literacy," and some people think about teaching how to use an atlas. Others will think about using computers. Following is a short discussion of terms people often think of as being the same as information literacy. They are perfectly good terms, but they are not information literacy.

Library Skills

Information literacy is not library instruction or library skills. Library skills focus on helping students understand how to use specific resources, that is, the mechanics of the resources. For example, students are taught how to use an encyclopedia, a poetry index, a magazine index, and the online catalog, as well as how to understand the Dewey Decimal System. Finding a few sources of information that could be used is the purpose of library skills. While information literacy skills do include accessing information, they go far beyond that, to using and thinking about information. The skills of evaluating the appropriateness of facts to the information need or problem, combining information into new knowledge, and communicating the new knowledge in an effective way are part of information literacy skills but not part of library skills.

Computer Literacy

Information literacy also is not the same as computer literacy. A library media specialist was introducing the new information literacy curriculum at a staff meeting. She explained that the library media specialists in the district had worked together to develop a K–12 articulated curriculum, using the student competencies listed in *Information Power: Building Partnerships for Learning* (AASL & AECT, 1998) and reviewing curricula from other school districts. The library media specialist then went over the major parts of the curriculum and reminded the teachers that the information literacy skills would be integrated into other curricula.

At the completion of her remarks a fifth-grade teacher raised her hand and said she felt her students were already information literate. She had them using the computer to answer questions all the time, and they did a good job. Having helped some of these students, the library media specialist knew they were basically filling out worksheets using the computer. An example of a question they answered was, "How many flags have flown over the state of Texas?" There was no thought involved and no application for this bit of information. Thinking about information and applying it are basic tenets of an information literate person. What the teacher was really saying was, "My students are computer literate." They knew how to use a computer to find information. They were not being taught how to use the information.

Computer literacy generally means that a person has keyboarding skills and ability in using the computer and in manipulating the software. Computer literacy is certainly necessary for students to become information literate. Computers assist in accessing information via the Internet and online databases, manipulation of data in spreadsheets or databases, and presentation of information through the use of word processors and PowerPoint™ or similar programs. The computer is a tool to facilitate learning. The superintendent and teacher mentioned above were confusing computer literacy with information literacy.

Digital Literacy

According to Eisenberg, Carrie, and Spitzer, digital literacy considers the broad range of resources that are accessible online and underscores the importance of looking at each of these resources with a critical eye (2004, p. 8). A digitally literate person will consider the author of the information a clue to the accuracy and bias of the information. Unlike books and magazines, which are overseen by editors, online resources can be posted by individuals without expertise in a given field. Because of the need to examine the authority, accuracy, and bias in online resources, digital literacy can be used in teaching information literacy.

Media Literacy

Media literacy is not the same as information literacy. A media literate student can critically analyze visual messages from billboards, signs, magazines, television, the Internet, and video and recognize the influence of those media on people. A media literate person understands that ads send subliminal messages about our culture and society. Those messages are meant to persuade the viewer to buy certain products. Media literacy is also important, but it is not a substitute for information literacy. Incorporating media literacy with information literacy provides students with another way to examine information.

Why Information Literacy?

Information by itself is of little value. It is not equal to knowledge. With the adoption of state standards, the ability to think critically and reason has become increasingly important. Unlike library skills, thinking and reasoning are exactly what information literacy instruction ensures. Information literacy is not a program or a technique, but rather a goal that reflects students' abilities to use information. It is mainly about developing understanding and insight. Information literacy instruction goes beyond memorizing facts to promoting research and understanding, understanding that is demonstrated through projects or products. Students must be involved with the information they find and must connect new information with what they already know (Doyle, 1994). Students gain proficiency in inquiry as they learn to interpret and use information (Kuhlthau, 1987). Information literacy skills help students convert information into understanding. Literacy is about interpretations of information to guide decisions, solve problems, and steer through uncertain, complex futures (McKenzie, 2000, p. 41). Information literacy skills help students filter out information that is not needed.

Information literacy can be thought of as combining the familiar library skills (location and access) with the process of learning from information (evaluating, using, synthesizing, and communicating). More access to information is not sufficient; students need the critical skills of sorting, evaluating, and using the information available (*Horace*, 1995). Instruction that helps students develop a realistic perception of an information system prepares them to be more successful searchers (Kuhlthau, 1987). To achieve proficiency in information literacy, instruction in a research process is needed.

Because literacy depends on information, and because information is expanding at an exponential rate, the mere ability to read and write must be being translated into the ability to read, write, and develop the capacities to understand, absorb, assimilate, and digest images being transmitted electronically, with the added capacity to communicate these images electrographically (Ross, Tweed & Bailey, 1994, reported in Langford, 1998, pp. 7–8). Not only is information expanding rapidly; with the advent of the Internet and the ease of creating Web pages, the accuracy of the information must be questioned. Unlike books and magazines, in which editorial constraints help to ensure the accuracy of the information being presented, anyone can publish a Web site. There is no assurance that a Web site has accurate information, or that the author knows anything about the subject. Consequently, students must be taught how to determine the value, accuracy, and bias of information.

Information literacy is important because students cannot be taught all they will possibly need to know to survive and succeed. The National Forum on Information Literacy (NFIL), which included 65 national organizations from business, government, and education, said in its final report that the dreams of a new and better tomorrow will only begin to be realized when all young people graduate into the workforce with strong information literacy skills (NFIL, 1998, reported in Spitzer, Eisenberg & Lowe, 1998, p. 40). The Partnership for 21st Century Skills has as its stated goal "to ensure that we measure the content and skills that will help prepare our students to meet the demands of the global community and tomorrow's workplace" (*Partnerships,* 2004). The organization has developed a series of Information and Communication Technology Literacy Maps (ICT) to show how ITC literacy intersects with core academic subjects. These are skills students need to enter the workplace:

1. Information and Communication Skills:

   - Information and Media Literacy: Analyzing, accessing, managing, integrating, evaluating and creating information in a variety of forms and media. Understanding the role of media in society.

   - Communication Skills: Understanding, managing and creating effective oral, written and multimedia communication in a variety of forms and contexts.

2. Thinking and Problem-solving Skills:

   - Critical Thinking and Systems Thinking: Exercising sound reasoning in understanding and making complex choices, understanding the interconnections among systems.

   - Problem identification, formulation and solution: Ability to frame, analyze and solve problems.

   - Creativity and intellectual curiosity: Developing, implementing and communicating new ideas to others, staying open and responsive to new and diverse perspectives.

3. Interpersonal and Self-Directional Skills:

   - Interpersonal and collaborative skills: Demonstrating teamwork and leadership; adapting to varied roles and responsibilities; working productively with others; exercising empathy; respecting diverse perspective.

• Self Direction: Monitoring one's own understanding and learning needs, locating appropriate resources, transferring learning from one domain to another.

• Accountability and Adaptability: Exercising personal responsibility and flexibility in personal, workplace and community contexts; setting and meeting high standards and goals for one's self and others; tolerating ambiguity.

• Social Responsibility: Acting responsibly with the interest of the larger community in mind; demonstrating ethical behavior in personal, workplace and community contexts. (*Partnerships*, 2004)

Not only has business identified skills students need, the Association of American Universities, in partnership with The Pew Charitable Trusts, have developed Standards for Success. The standards are what students need to know to be successful at the college and university level. The Standards for Success goals follow:

1. Identify what students need to know and be able to do in order to succeed in entry-level university courses. Knowledge and Skills for University Success is a comprehensive and thoroughly grounded set of standards for college success

2. Produce a database of information on state high school assessments to improve the connection between the content of high school tests and the standards for university. (Understanding University Success, 2003)

Some information literacy skills are listed as standards students need in addition to specific subject area knowledge. Information literacy standards include identifying and organizing what is known and not known in a problem; the ability to find information from a variety of sources and be able to assess the quality and reliability of that information; and knowing a variety of note-taking methods for both research and class lectures.

In order to lead productive, interesting, and stimulating lives, students will need the skills to find, access, evaluate, and communicate information. Information literacy is a set of competencies that will remain with students throughout their lives. Regardless of the definition used, the literature is clear that all students must become information literate to become life-long learners.

Information Fluency

Daniel Callison takes the use of information literacy to the next level by including it as a part of information fluency. Information fluency involves the abilities to

- transfer information and media literacy skills to address new information need situations;

- employ the use of modern computer technologies to obtain, select, analyze, and infer conclusions from information;

- employ critical thinking to derive evidence from information and creative thinking for the expression and application of that evidence to decision-making; and

- move across multiple strategies and evaluation levels in order to address different information needs found in academic, workplace, and personal environments. (2003b, pp. 38–39)

An information fluent person knows how to use more than one research process and chooses the one that can best meet the information need in a given situation. (A discussion of research processes is in Chapter 7.) Computer literacy is more than knowing how to use a computer; it is being able to use the computer to analyze information and make inferences. An information fluent person can take from information literacy, computer literacy, media literacy, and digital literacy the appropriate aspects of each and meld them together to meet a particular information need in a specific situation.

Conclusion

Computer literacy, digital literacy, media literacy, and other types of literacy are all important skills to use in learning. However, the terms should not be used as synonyms for information literacy. Information literacy is the ability to recognize a need, then access, find, evaluate, use, and communicate information. This definition has evolved over the years and will continue to change as information needs change. Students living in the age of information overload and instant access to all types of information need to know how to deal with it all. Since information does not equal knowledge, students must learn not only how to find the information, but also how to evaluate and use it. Students must think about what they learn in terms of what they already know and turn that into new learning and knowledge. Finally, students must be able to communicate the new knowledge to others, for new knowledge does no one any good if it is not shared.

To be information literate is to be empowered. Bombarded by headline news, sound bites, and short written articles, people are encouraged to accept the opinions of others without much thought. Even the analysis after a presidential speech discourages thinking as the newscasters tell us what the president really said. Thomas Jefferson felt that an educated populace was vital to the survival of a democracy. If people have the ability to find information, think about it, and apply it to known situations, they can more readily make their own decisions and develop their own opinions. Information literacy skills have become needed survival skills in the 21st century.

CHAPTER 2

Information Literacy Standards

Many teachers and administrators tend to think of information literacy as the traditional library skills of finding and accessing information. The growth in the quantity of information and the ease of access demands that students have skills beyond location and access. They need information literacy skills that focus on a process of learning rather than the dissemination of information. The goal of information literacy is to prepare students to be effective users of information throughout their lives.

From Library Skills to Information Literacy

For decades school librarians taught students how to find resources. What students did with those resources was directed by the classroom teacher. The librarian focused on teaching the Dewey Decimal System; how to find materials on the shelves; how to use the card catalog and all its rules; and how to use certain tools such as encyclopedias, dictionaries, and *The Reader's Guide to Periodical Literature*. Although this information was valuable to students, librarians were only teaching part of what was needed. Instruction was usually done without much thought about what was going on in the classroom. Librarians taught lessons in isolation and on a fixed schedule. For example, in September a librarian might teach how to use the encyclopedia. Every year using the encyclopedia was taught in September, with little thought given to whether students needed to know how to use the encyclopedia. In fact, whether students ever used the encyclopedia was often left to the classroom teacher.

Teaching library skills in isolation began to change in 1988 with the publication of *Information Power: Guidelines for School Library Media Programs*. The mission of the library media program became making students and staff effective users of ideas and information (AASL & AECT, 1988). To accomplish

13

this mission, library media specialists were to provide intellectual access to information through systematic learning activities that develop cognitive strategies for selecting, retrieving, analyzing, evaluating, synthesizing, and creating information at all age levels and in all curriculum content areas (AASL & AECT, 1988, p. 1).

With the publication of *Information Power: Building Partnerships for Learning* (AASL & AECT, 1998), the focus shifted from teaching location and access to teaching about information. Accessing and finding resources was still being taught, but the scope of instruction was expanded to include what to do with the information once it was found, that is, using, synthesizing, and communicating information. Not only had the scope of the content changed, the content was to be integrated with other curricula. No longer was the use of the encyclopedia to be taught just because it was September. Instead, teaching students how the encyclopedia was organized and how to use the index, as well as when to use the encyclopedia, was done when students had a reason to use it.

The difference between library skills and information literacy skills is illustrated in Figure 2.1.

Library Skills	*Information Literacy*
Skills taught in isolation	Skills integrated with other curricula
Skills taught on specific schedule	Skills taught when needed
Emphasis on locating and accessing resources	Emphasis on evaluating and using resources
	Learn search strategies
LMS makes all decisions	Collaboration with classroom teacher
LMS responsible for learning	Student responsible for learning
LMS directed	Student more self-directed
Printed resources	Resources in many formats
Evaluation of product	Evaluation, including self-evaluation, of process and product

Figure 2.1. Comparison of Library Skills and Information Literacy Skills.

Information Literacy Standards

What abilities are needed for everyday life in an information society? Sternberg (1985, reported in Doyle, 1994) found that the first and most difficult step in problem solving was the ability to recognize that a problem exists and to define it. Sternberg further stated that in order to bridge the gaps that exist between the school and the real world, a process of information literacy should include identifying the problem, formulating a search strategy, acquiring resources, and evaluating the information to determine whether it solves the problem. *Information Power: Building Partnerships for Learning* (AASL & AECT, 1998) introduced nine information literacy standards that encompassed Sternberg's suggestions.

Perkins (1999) discusses the three roles in constructivism as the active learner, the social learner, and the creative learner. The active learner actively acquires knowledge and understanding. Students discuss, debate, hypothesize, investigate, and take viewpoints. The social learner sees knowledge and understanding as socially constructed. Knowledge and understanding are constructed by interacting with others. The creative learner creates or re-creates knowledge and understanding. For example, the learner is guided by teachers to rediscover scientific theories and historical perspectives.

Langford (1998) argues that the term *information literacy* is unclear because the desired outcomes are unclear. The nine literacy standards developed by the American Association of School Librarians (AASL) and the Association of Educational Communications Technology (AECT) and published in *Information Power: Building Partnerships for Learning* (1988) answer Langford's concern that information literacy standards are unclear. These standards also fit with Perkins's description of constructivism. Further, the standards agree with cognitive psychologists' definition of learning as actively building knowledge through interaction with information and experiences.

AASL & AECT Information Literacy Standards

The nine AASL & AECT standards are categorized under three headings: Information Literacy, Independent Learning, and Social Responsibility. Each heading contains three standards:

Information Literacy

1. The student who is information literate accesses information efficiently and effectively.

2.   The student who is information literate evaluates information critically and competently.

3.   The student who is information literate uses information accurately and creatively.

Independent Learning Standards

4.   The student who is an independent learner is information literate and pursues information related to personal interests.

5.   The student who is an independent learner is information literate and appreciates literature and other creative expressions of information.

6.   The student who is an independent learner is information literate and strives for excellence in information seeking and knowledge generation.

Social Responsibility Standards

7.   The student who contributes positively to the learning community and to society is information literate and recognizes the importance of information to a democratic society.

8.   The student who contributes positively to the learning community and to society is information literate and practices ethical behavior in regard to information and information technology.

9.   The student who contributes positively to the learning community and to society is information literate and participates effectively in groups to pursue and generate information. (AASL & AECT, 1998, pp. 8–9)

Each standard has indicators and three levels of proficiency. For example, Standard 1: "The student who is information literate accesses information efficiently and effectively," has as its first indicator "Recognizes the need for information." A complete list of the standards and their indicators can be found on the AASL Web site (http://www.ala.org/ala/aasl/aaslindex.htm).

Information Literacy Standards at the Local Level

The AASL & AECT information literacy standards are broad general student outcomes that describe an information literate student. Performance indicators, levels of proficiency, and examples are provided with the standards. Chapter 3 of this book focuses on the process of aligning national and state standards with local curriculum. In this chapter the focus is on what information literacy skills look like at the local level. The library media specialist and some classroom teachers need to translate the AASL & AECT information literacy standards and indicators into standards and indicators appropriate for their learning community.

At the local level, library media specialists should keep in mind that "[i]nstruction that helps them *(students)* develop a realistic perception of an information system prepares them to be more successful searchers" (Kuhlthau, 1987, p. 26). Students should be able to distinguish useful information from the irrelevant. "Information skills are not isolated incidents, but rather connected activities that encompass a way of thinking about and using information" (Eisenberg & Berkowitz, 1999, p. 5). As the first three standards are discussed, a similarity to several process-based approaches to research, such as the Big6™, Flip It!™, and others, can be seen. The difference is that standards are what library media specialists use to measure students' competencies, whereas the research process is how students gain the competencies. Some common research processes are discussed in Chapter 7.

Standard 1, accessing information efficiently and effectively, includes recognizing the need for information, formulating questions, and locating resources. Providing questions that require students to use higher order thinking skills is critical. Low-level fact-finding questions are not sufficient beyond a beginning level. Low-level fact-finding questions are often basic, for example, "What do sea horses eat?" or "What was the Stamp Act?" This type of question is appropriate for first graders who are beginning researchers. High school students will use low-level fact-finding questions when they begin research on a topic about which they know little. As students gain proficiency in researching they need to move beyond low-level fact-finding questions to build their own questions that will motivate them to find the answers.

In order to build their own questions students need time to read, view, or listen to sources of information. They need time to think about what they already know about a topic and relate it to what they have just read in order to develop meaningful research questions. Without time to read, students often do not know enough about a topic to ask questions of interest to them. Hurrying at this point deprives the student of quality interaction time with the resources and results in trivial questions requiring little critical thinking.

Standard 2, evaluating information critically and competently, is important in light of the amount of information that is available today. When using a book a student is usually assured that the information has been written and edited by knowledgeable people. The same cannot be said about all electronic sources, especially those available on the Internet. Students must be able to determine the accuracy and relevance of information; distinguish among fact, point of view, and opinion; identify inaccurate and misleading information; and find information that answers the research question.

Some schools use a handout to help students determine the credibility of Web sites. Web evaluation criteria vary from school to school but often include the author's credentials and affiliation, title of the work, whether or not sources of information are stated, date of creation or modification, and URL. The scope of the work is important. Is the purpose stated? Are the facts indeed facts, or just opinions? Students must be taught to look for key words or phrases, such as "in my opinion," or "everyone agrees that" in order to identify a possible bias. Is the information useful? Students have to be taught that not all information, although interesting, is pertinent to their topic.

Some Internet search engines are quite sophisticated. Before students have developed search strategies and the skills to determine good Internet sites, teachers may want to limit students to using pre-selected sites. The pre-selected site could be a bookmark or be put on the school's Web site. There are Web site available to teachers on which they can set up pages for students to access. A common one is TrackStar. Using online subscription databases is another way to help students develop a sense of how good online resources can be.

Under Standard 3 a student uses information accurately and creatively. The student knows and uses different ways to organize information, integrates what is known with new knowledge, applies critical thinking and problem solving, and communicates the results in an appropriate format. The emphasis in this standard is on thinking: thinking in new ways, applying known information in different ways, using information to draw conclusions and develop new understandings. Critical thinking and problem solving are important.

Critical thinking lies between believing everything that is read and believing nothing that is read. When students think critically, they apply criteria to judge information for accuracy, authority, and relevance to the problem. To foster critical thinking, library media specialists and teachers must ask probing questions: why, how, and what difference does the information make? Students will learn to take information from a variety of sources and apply it to a given problem.

Students need to experience communicating the results of their learning in a variety of formats so they can begin to develop a sense of which communication tool is best in any given situation. Sometimes teachers will determine what method of communication will be used, by the amount of computer time available or the need to do more writing. The method may also be determined by the fact that students have not had experience in a given communication tool. For example, in one school a project that required an oral presentation was developed for third graders because fourth graders were not doing well on the oral presentation standard that was evaluated at the beginning of the school year. The library media specialist worked with the students on the project, and in particular on what made a good oral presentation. By doing this project at the end of third grade, the students had one more experience in giving oral presentations before they had to meet the state standard (Joyce Udey and Lori Hess, personal communication, March 2004). While teacher determination of the method of presentation is fine at times, as students become proficient in several communication tools, they must take some responsibility in choosing an appropriate method to present the information.

Independent Learner Standards at the Local Level

An independent learner, according to Standard 4, pursues information related to personal interests. Students seek information related to areas such as careers, hobbies, health matters, and environmental issues of interest. Then, information is produced and solutions are designed, developed, and evaluated related to those personal interests.

Personal interest is a huge motivational factor for students finding information. From the third-grade student who wanted to know if there are male and female butterflies to the senior making decisions about what college to attend, the key factor is a personal interest or need to know. The freshman and sophomore history classes in the Columbus, Nebraska, High School learned that the man responsible for designing and building the boat that allowed the allied troops to land on D-Day was born in their home town. The teacher wondered why nothing had ever been done to recognize Andrew Jackson Higgins and asked the classes if they would be interested in doing something to honor him. From that innocent beginning came a multi-year project in which students researched Higgins, his company, and where his boat had been used. They designed a memorial, contacted local businesses to support them, carried out fund-raising activities, and wrote letters to prominent people such as the governor and state and national representatives. Part of the memorial was to contain sand from all the beaches on which the Higgins boats landed. The students found individuals who were willing to see they got the sand. Students wrote the inscriptions that are a part of the memorial. When it came time to dedicate the first phase of the memorial, the students contacted Mr. Higgins's daughters and invited them to be a part of the ceremony. Today, as a result of student interest and motivation to research a problem and find an answer, the city has a national monument to Andrew Jackson Higgins. Motivation is powerful.

Appreciation of literature and other creative expressions of information are the heart of Standard 5. Indicators include being a competent and self-motivated reader, the ability to derive information from a variety of formats, and success in creating products in a variety of formats.

Appreciation of literature can be exhibited in different ways. A young child can tell you his or her favorite part of a story, while older students can discuss complex ideas and compare them to other works of literature. Children who read a lot are usually self-motivated readers. The non-motivated readers are the ones library media specialists work hard to reach. Many schools have reading incentive programs to encourage students to read. There may be time set aside during the day for all students and teachers to read, or there may be a program in which students read at home and parents must sign a form stating that the students read for the required amount of time.

A critical element in literature appreciation is having a library media center with books on a variety of topics, in different formats (books, magazines, comic books), and on different reading levels. Graphic novels have become more popular with reluctant readers. Lance and others (1993) found that students performed better on academic tests when library media collections contained large amounts of quality materials, including print and multimedia. More resources make for better readers, but those resources must be of interest to students.

Under Standard 6 the student is to strive for excellence in information seeking and knowledge generation. Assessing the quality of the process and the product and revising, improving, and updating self-generated knowledge accomplish this standard. For many students the goal is to get done; to finish the assignment and move on. Under Standard 6 students must learn that they have to continually look at the research process to make sure they have the information they need. If they don't, the students then have to revisit the appropriate step and find further information, rethink their conclusion, or revise the product. A sophisticated, information literate student learns that revision is the norm, not the exception.

Student self-evaluation is an important part of this standard. The first question that students often have to ask regarding the final product is, "Did I answer the question?" If not, what additional information do they need? While doing the research students should ask themselves, "Does this information answer one of my questions?" Elementary students have a difficult time limiting themselves to recording just information that pertains to the problem or question they are answering. This lack of experience is why helping them develop good questions is important.

Other questions for students to ask might be, "Is this the best way to share the information?" "Do I have the skills to develop the product I want?" "Is the type of presentation appropriate for the audience?" Students need models of what good presentations are. They need to see good examples of oral reports, PowerPoint presentations, dioramas, and posters.

Social Responsibility Standards at the Local Level

Standard 7 requires that the student understand the importance of information to a democratic society. Information is sought from different sources, contexts, and cultures. Further, the student respects the principle of equitable access to information. At the highest level of competency, students are concerned that everyone have access to information and information technology.

The library media specialist should not only provide resources with different points of view, representing different cultures, and in different formats, but also encourage students to use them. Sometimes this may mean requiring students to use a videotape or interview a community member. Ultimately students should be able to determine which type of resource is best for a given information problem and recognize that not all people look at a problem in the same way. For example, a community may need a by-pass around the city because many large trucks are going through town. The problem students need to solve is where the by-pass should go. Teams of students could be assigned to research the problem, develop a solution, and present it to the appropriate decision-making group. (The decision-making group can be a mock group rather than an actual one.) The teams would take the point of view of one of the following groups: business owners, truck drivers, the Chamber of Commerce, the city council, property owners whose land might be taken, or residents of the city. Because the points of view of the groups are different, the information they need and gather will be different, as will the factors they consider. Their conclusions should also be different.

Although library media specialists have always been concerned about responsible use of information, the teaching of ethical use of information has not always been stressed. Under Standard 8 the student practices ethical behavior in regard to information and information technology. The student respects intellectual property rights and uses information technology responsibly.

At a very basic level, students should be able to define intellectual property rights. Second grade is not too early to begin teaching students to respect these rights. Second graders understand the concept of stealing, and discussing how they would feel if they wrote something and someone else stole it and said they wrote it has meaning to them. As students progress in their understanding, they can be introduced to the term *plagiarism* and the idea of respecting the work of others. Ultimately students should be able to explain what would happen in a society in which intellectual property rights were not respected.

Students must be required to cite all Internet and online databases they use. Likewise, any presentations made using presentation tools such as PowerPoint must contain a bibliography. If students use pictures from the Internet, they must be cited. From about third grade on up students should begin to understand that there is a difference in what they can copy and use in a class project and what they can copy and give to friends.

Introducing the idea of respecting the work of others can begin as early as kindergarten by having students write on projects that they got their information from a book. Usually the library media specialist will write, "I got my information from" and the student will then write the word "book." As students advance through the grades they begin to write bibliographies by compiling simple ones that include only the authors and titles of books. Gradually additional components are included, until as high school students they can complete a fairly sophisticated bibliography. Ideally, regardless of the bibliographic format being used, it should be standard throughout the school, K–12.

Finally, Standard 9 focuses on students participating effectively in groups to pursue and generate information. Students demonstrate this standard by sharing knowledge and information with others; respecting others' ideas and acknowledging their contributions; collaborating with others to identify information problems and seek solutions; and collaborating with others to design, develop, and evaluate information products and solutions.

Primary students demonstrate this standard when they share something they have learned with a fellow student or show an interesting picture. High school students share Web sites with each other. At a higher level, students can design sophisticated hypermedia presentations together. The students involved in the by-pass project mentioned in the discussion of Standard 7 would be working in groups, sharing ideas and information, and reaching a decision together. They also have to develop a product to persuade another group to adopt their solution. The experience acquired in defining an information problem, researching it, developing a solution, and presenting it in a group situation is a skill that students will use throughout their lives.

Conclusion

The development of the nine information literacy standards was an important milestone in advancing the teaching of information literacy. As library media specialists work together and with classroom teachers, these standards become a framework for them to follow. Each school district should adapt the AASL & AECT standards to fit state and local standards. The standards go beyond the teaching of a research process to encompass the ethical use of information and recognizing that students need to become sophisticated consumers of information found in different formats, written from different points of view, and reflecting different cultures. Further, communicating what has been learned in an appropriate format is vital. Students today have a wide variety of communication options and must be able to select the appropriate ones for each audience.

CHAPTER 3

Putting It All Together: National, State, and Local Standards

Standards are a fact of life in education today. They tell teachers and library media specialists exactly what essential skills and knowledge students should learn. Most national associations have developed standards for specific subject areas. National curriculum guidelines and standards recognize the importance of learning concepts, skills, and attitudes rather than memorizing individual facts.

Almost all states have written standards for students to achieve in at least some subject areas. State standards are often written using the national ones as guidelines. At the local level school districts must align their curricula to the state standards. Information literacy skills are unique in that not only must local, state, and national information literacy standards be aligned, but the local information literacy skills must also be integrated with all other curricula. "It is the way standards are utilized that will dictate the quality of education, not the fact of their existence" (Allen, 1999).

Information Literacy Standards: State

As discussed in Chapter 2, national standards for information literacy have been developed by the AASL and AECT. Although the national standards are not mandated, they have been used by states and local school districts to develop their own information literacy standards. Some states mandate information literacy standards. Colorado, for example, has adopted the national standards and provided appropriate assessment. Wisconsin has developed a set of information literacy skills based on the national standards. Other states, such as Nebraska, have imbedded a single standard within another curriculum. Finally, there are states in which no information literacy standards exist.

Examples of State Standards

California

The California School Library Association has developed a 12-stage process for information literacy standards:

1. Explore/Identify the need for information

2. Formulate the central search question

3. Relate question to previous knowledge and identify key words, concepts, and names

4. Identify potential resources

5. Develop general search strategies to organize the search

6. Locate and explore previously identified resources

7. Select most useful resources and formulate specific strategies for using them

8. Search for relevant information

9. Evaluate, select, and organize information

10. Analyze information retrieved: interpret, infer, and integrate

11. Determine how to use/present/communicate information: organize information for intended use/ use information

12. Evaluate results; evaluate process. (California School Library Association, 1997, pp. 21–27)

Colorado

Colorado has developed information literacy standards that closely follow the national guidelines developed by AASL and AECT. This example includes Colorado's first three standards:

The information literate student . . .

> STANDARD 1 . . . accesses information efficiently and effectively
>
> STANDARD 2 . . . evaluates information critically and competently
>
> STANDARD 3 . . . uses information accurately and creatively. (Colorado Department of Education, 2002, p. 1)

Each of the nine standards has a rationale and indicators similar to the state's classroom standards. An assessment is given for each standard. For example, the assessment guidelines for Standard 1, access information efficiently and effectively, include the following:

- States overview of a topic
- Connects ideas and other issues to a main topic
- States more than one side to an issue
- Indicates when information is complete or incomplete; accurate or inaccurate
- Develops essential questions that go beyond facts and are thoughtful
- Locates information using a variety of formats
- Identifies and uses primary and secondary sources
- Locates relevant information to answer research questions. (Colorado Department of Education, 2002)

Nebraska

In Nebraska, one information literacy standard was written and included in the Reading/Writing Standards that were developed for grades 4, 8, and 12. The information literacy standards are the following:

> By the end of the fourth grade, students will identify the resource appropriate for a specific purpose, and use the resource to locate information.
>
> By the end of the eighth grade, students will identify, locate, and use multiple resources to access information on an assigned or self-selected topic.

By the end of the twelfth grade, students will locate, evaluate, and use primary and secondary resources for research. (Nebraska Department of Education, 2001, pp. 3, 6, 9)

Each grade level has several example indicators to be used to develop local assessments. These indicators include statements such as the following:

- Use general reference materials (dictionary, thesaurus, encyclopedia, atlas, telephone book, almanac)

- Use electronic resources (CD-ROM, software programs, online resources)

- Use library resources (card or electronic catalog, periodicals, and other informational text).

- Use multimedia resources (video/audio tapes)

- Use print reference materials (gazetteer, atlas, specialized index, handbook, manual, government document, book of quotations, college and career resources, and citation style manual).

- Identify and gather resources that provide relevant and reliable information. (Nebraska Department of Education, 2001, pp. 3, 6, 9)

In Nebraska each school district develops its own set of assessment tools for the core subject (reading/writing, science, math, and social studies), so how the standards are evaluated varies from district to district.

Wisconsin

Wisconsin developed four content standards for information literacy that were designed to be integrated into various content and skill areas. The four standards use media and technology to access, organize, create, and communicate information for solving problems and constructing new knowledge, products, and systems:

1. [S]elect and use media and technology to access, organize, create, and communicate information for solving problems and constructing new knowledge, products, and systems.

2. [A]ccess, evaluate, and apply information efficiently and effectively from a variety of sources in print, nonprint, and electronic formats to meet personal and academic needs.

3. [A]pply information and technology skills to issues of personal and academic interest by actively and independently seeking information; demonstrating critical and discriminating reading, listening, and viewing habits; and, striving for personal excellence in learning and career pursuits.

4. [D]emonstrate the ability to work collaboratively in teams or groups, use information and technology in a responsible manner, respect intellectual property rights, and recognize the importance of intellectual freedom and access to information in a democratic society. (Wisconsin Association of School Librarians, 2000, pp. 156, 221, 345, 443)

For each of the content standards, performance standards have been developed for grades 4, 8, and 12. Each performance standard has several indicators.

Information Literacy Standards: Local

Locally, information literacy standards have to be considered on two levels. First, a district or school must have its own information literacy skills. Second, the information literacy skills must be correlated or integrated with other curricular standards. Information literacy instruction affects test scores. A study conducted in Alaska showed that the more often students receive information literacy instruction in which the library media center staff are involved, the higher their test scores are (Lance & Loertscher, 2003).

Creating Local Standards

Library media specialists at the local level must take a leadership role in seeing that information literacy skills are developed. That leadership begins with knowing what that state's and the national standards are for information literacy. Having access to examples from other school districts is useful. Having gathered the appropriate resources and considered ahead of time whom to involve in the development of the standards and what process might be used, the library media specialist is ready to approach the administration. Gaining administrative support is critical, for without that support the time to develop the standards and the credibility given to them by other staff members will be minimal.

Certain questions must be addressed when developing local standards.

Who Will Define the Local Standards?

Will the library media specialist develop the standards alone? This is not a recommended procedure. Which classroom teachers will be involved? The climate and structure of the school will be a factor here. In elementary schools it is often necessary to include representatives from both primary and upper grades. At the high school all department heads may have to be involved in order for the standards to gain acceptance. Within any school there is sometimes a leader who is critical to the acceptance of any change, and that person should be included. This leader may or may not be a department head or the teacher with the most seniority. Should the teacher who is most likely to resist standards be included on the team? Sometimes this type of person provides an alternate viewpoint that is worth considering. Is the principal or curriculum director to be included? Again, this decision depends on the structure of the school. Some districts will require that an administrator be included.

What Process Will Be Used to Develop the Standards?

Does the school district have a model it has used to develop other curricular standards? If so, it might be a good idea to use it or at least adapt it. If not, the following questions can be used as a guide for developing a process.

Are the standards to be district or building standards?

Answering this question will provide some insight into who should be on the team. If the standards are being written for the district, representatives from the elementary, middle, and high schools should be included. Both classroom teachers and library media specialists should be represented, as well as the administration. One or two community members may also be included.

Have standards already been developed that can be adapted?

Be familiar with national and state standards for information literacy. Have copies of what other states have done. Some states have outlines of information standards available on a Web site. Some organizations, such as the Wisconsin Association of School Librarians, have documents for sale.

In what format will the standards be written?

If the school has written other curricular standards, have copies of them so the information literacy format can be patterned after them. If the school has no format to use, examine what other schools or states have done. Also, consider what is useful to the teachers and to the library media staff. For example, do you want a three-ring notebook format?

What terminology will be used?

Adopting existing local terminology is not only expedient but ensures consistency among the different standards. Staff members do not have to learn a new set of terms just for information literacy. Terms such as *benchmarks, indicators,* and *performance standards* are common. Examining what other schools have done will provide some useful examples.

At what grade level and subject areas will benchmarks be established?

Here state and local district requirements will have to be followed. If the state and school district have benchmarks at grades 4, 8, and 12, then the information literacy skills should follow that policy. Describe the expected levels of performance and indicators for each benchmark.

How will standards be assessed, and who will do it?

Some states have defined assessments that all schools must follow. If this is the case, the information literacy standards should follow the same type of assessment. Some states go so far as to develop assessments for each standard. Library media specialists should be aware of whether such assessments exist and if they are required or merely suggested. Does the local school district require that assessments be developed for all standards? Is there a preferred format such as rubrics? The team integrating the information literacy standards with the other curricula should be aware of what the local requirement for assessment of standards is. Schools in Nebraska are allowed to write their own assessments. One school uses the Iowa Tests of Basic Skills (ITBS) as a measurement of meeting the standards. The Reference Materials section of the ITBS is used to test how well students do in the area of information literacy skills. The students do well on the tests, but only a portion of what is being taught is tested. The library media specialists would say that the process of finding, evaluating, using, and communicating information is the focus of the curriculum, not whether students can use the table of contents, important as that skill may be.

If assessments must be developed, the national standards and some state standards have levels of proficiencies that can be used as a starting point. A related question concerning the information literacy skills is who will do the assessment. The library media specialist may not always be the most appropriate person, especially if the skill is tied closely to another content area standard. In some instances both the library media specialist and the classroom teacher may be involved in the assessment. Spelling out who does the assessment may have to be added to the integration document.

Who has the final authority on the local standards?

To whom do the standards have to be presented for approval? Is there a hierarchy of approval? Some schools have administrative teams or administrative cabinets that have to approve the standards before they are presented to the school board. In most cases the local school board will adopt the standards and the accompanying assessments. For this reason, including a representative from the school board on the development team might be a wise move.

Who needs a copy of the standards?

Finally, after the standards are completed and officially adopted, who should be given copies? Obviously the library media specialists and classroom teachers should have a copy. Do all teachers and library media specialists need a copy of the entire document, K–12, or just the portion that affects them? What about the administrators and school board members? Is there a district professional library that should have a copy? A school may already have an informal policy about how distribution of curriculum guides is done. This could be a starting place for deciding who gets copies of the standards.

Integrating with Other Curricula

When the process of developing the information standards begins, all stakeholders must understand that development is only part of the process. The second half of the process is the integration of the information literacy standards with other curricular areas. Not all participants will understand this need, and it may be necessary to spend some time educating them about the value of the integration. Some of the information discussed in Chapter 8 may be useful at this stage.

The library media specialist must take the lead in seeing that the integration takes place, especially in those curricula for which standards have been developed. The role of the library media specialist is to show how information literacy can help students be successful in meeting content area standards. To do this the library media specialist must be familiar with other curricula. One way to learn the curricula is to become part of curriculum development teams, even if the library media specialist has to initiate the idea. The time for sitting and waiting to be asked to be a part of curriculum teams is over. Becoming involved may also mean participating in various training and staff development, both as a participant and a presenter. Seizing every opportunity to learn more about curriculum, how students learn, and standards is critical if information literacy standards are to be integrated at the local level.

Integrating information literacy standards and other curricula standards is a time-consuming process, as each curriculum standard must be read to see what information literacy standard, if any, fits with it. Information literacy skills do not have to be integrated into every curriculum at the same time, or even in the same year. Work with the curriculum revision cycle in the school and do the correlations or integration as a particular curriculum is revised. In the meantime, library media specialists can work with teachers in the classroom to see where skills best fit. They can meet with teachers, individually or in teams, to plan where to teach which skill. For example, the library media specialist and a teacher might identify where some information literacy skills will fit within the social studies curriculum. This information can then be used when the time comes to correlate the information literacy skills with the social studies curriculum. If teachers know the information literacy objectives, they understand better how to use the library media specialist's expertise.

How does one actually go about integrating two curriculum areas? Looking for some key words in the subject area curriculum standards can be a starting place. In the following science standard, the sample indicators use the words "research and report" or "research and describe," which are logical points at which to suggest using information literacy standards to help the student meet the expected outcome:

> ***The Standard:*** The history and nature of science illustrates different aspects of scientific inquiry, the human aspects of science, and the role of science in the development of various cultures.
>
> ***The Benchmark:*** By the end of fourth grade, students will develop an understanding of science as a human endeavor.
>
> ***Sample Indicators***
>
> - Research and report on the contributions to science and technology throughout history by men and women scientists of diverse cultures.
>
> - Research and report on how science is used in different careers.
>
> - Research and report on how current scientific discoveries illustrate that science is an ongoing process.
>
> ***Benchmark:*** By the end of eighth grade, students will develop an understanding of the history of science.

Sample Indicator:

- Research and describe the difficulties experienced by scientific innovators who had to overcome commonly held
  beliefs of their times to reach conclusions that we now
  take for granted.

Benchmark: By the end of twelfth grade, students will develop
an understanding of the history of science.

Sample Indicator:

- Investigate and describe the contributions of diverse cultures to scientific knowledge and technological inven-
  tions. (Nebraska Department of Education, 2001, pp. 7,
  13, 20)

It will be necessary to develop a format to show how the subject area
standards and information literacy skills standards relate to each other. There
are many ways to do this. Figure 3.1 shows a simple way to demonstrate the
relationship between state science standards and national information literacy
standards.

By taking the initiative, the library media specialist can show classroom
teachers how using some of the information literacy objectives can help students master the science standard. In the eighth grade standard in Figure 3.1,
the sample indicator is, "Research and report on the difficulties experienced
by a scientific innovator who had to overcome flawed, commonly held beliefs
of his or her time to reach conclusions that we now take for granted." There
are several information literacy skills that could be taught here. For example,
the standard of accessing information efficiently and effectively could be
used. One of the indicators for this standard is "formulates questions based on
information needs" (AASL & AECT, 1998). The library media specialist
could explain to the students that developing the questions will help them focus on what they need to learn, for example, what people believed, rather than
when the scientist was born and where he or she went to school.

Nebraska Science Standards	AASL/AECT Information Literacy Standards for Student Learning
First Grade: 1.2.1 Develop the abilities needed to do scientific inquiry.	1.1 Recognizes the need for information. 1.3 Formulates questions based on information needs. 1.5 Develops and uses successful strategies for locating information. 2.4 Selects information appropriate to the problems or question at hand.
Fourth Grade: 4.1.2 Develop an understanding of evidence, models, and explanations.	2.1 Determines accuracy, relevance, and comprehensiveness. 2.2 Distinguishes among fact, point of view, and opinion. 2.3 Identifies inaccurate and misleading information.
Eighth Grade: 8.8.3 Develop an understanding of the history of science * Research and report on the difficulties experienced by a scientific innovator who had to overcome flawed, commonly held beliefs of his or her time to reach conclusions that we now take for granted.	3.1 Organizes information for practical application. 3.2 Integrates new information into one's own knowledge. 3.3 Applies information in critical thinking and problem solving. 3.4 Produces and communicates information and ideas in appropriate formats
Twelfth Grade: 12.5.4 Develop a scientific understanding of the origin of the universe. *Research and describe the life cycle of a star. *Research and understand that changes in scientific knowledge evolve over time and almost always build on earlier knowledge.	2.1 Determines accuracy, relevance, and comprehensiveness. 2.2 Distinguishes among fact, point of view, and opinion. 2.3 Identifies inaccurate and misleading information. 2.4 Selects information appropriate to the problem or question at hand. 9.1 Shares knowledge and information with others.

Figure 3.1. Correlation of State and National Standards (Nebraska Educational Media Association, 1999).

Conclusion

Standards tell educators what the essential learning skills are. Indicators are used to show teachers and library media specialists what to observe or what students should be able to do in order to meet the standards. Since not all students perform at the same level, performance levels are sometimes developed. These are useful in developing rubrics or other assessment tools.

Library media specialists need not be afraid of standards, but they should take the initiative to see that information literacy skills become a part of other curricula. To do this they must be knowledgeable about not only information literacy skills but also other curricula. There are a number of resources available to assist in the process of correlation of standards and information literacy. Among these are standards from various states and school districts as well as the national standards. Perhaps one of the best resources is another library media specialist who has been through the process.

"Ultimately, information literate people are those who have learned how to learn. They know how to learn because they know how knowledge is organized, how to find information in such a way that others can learn from them. They are people who are prepared for lifelong learning, because they can always find the information needed for any task or decision at hand" (American Library Association, 1989). This statement reflects the goal of integrating information literacy standards with other curricular standards.

CHAPTER 4

Planning for Information Literacy Instruction

What does information literacy look like at the local level? How does the library media specialist get an information literacy program started? There is no single answer, because much depends on whether or not there are state information literacy standards, the missions of the school district and the library media program, and the history and culture of the school. In this chapter some rationale and methods that others have used are presented.

Generally the library media specialist starts the process for developing and integrating information literacy skills. The library media specialist usually sees the need for such skills and has a commitment to meet students' needs. Armed with evidence of the need for information literacy at the building level and with research such as that reported by Lance and Loertscher (2003) showing the importance of such skills in academic achievement, the library media specialist begins to develop the support of the building principal. To build that support Hartzell (1994) suggests the following:

- Take the initiative instead of waiting for the principal to come to you. If you wait the principal may never come.

- Do your homework before going to see the principal. When you go to the principal with a problem, have solutions.

- Be your own publicist and promoter, but be subtle.

- Talk to people before you talk to the principal. You need to know what research supports and what teachers are thinking. Know how what you want to do will affect students.

- Don't get caught up in jargon or titles. Use straightforward language.

As an instructional partner, the library media specialist must join with teachers and others to identify links across student information needs, curricular content, learning outcomes, and a wide variety of resources (AASL &

AECT, 1998). To accomplish this the library media specialist must be a change agent, leader, pedagogical innovator, and risk taker.

The Process

Having gained the support of the principal, the library media specialist can put in place a process to develop a building level information literacy curriculum. The key to a successful process, adoption, and implementation lies in involving classroom teachers as well as the administrator. Without the involvement of others, the information literacy curriculum belongs solely to the library media specialist. For other teachers to buy into the curriculum, they must be a part of the planning process.

A number of processes can be used. The process chosen will vary by school district. Some school districts take existing local curriculum and correlate it with state standards. Others develop local standards as a process. Spitzer (1999) suggests the following steps in creating a plan for information literacy:

1. What is the definition of information literacy? Everyone involved must know what is meant by information literacy. The same definition must be used throughout the school and district.

2. Should implementing the Information Literacy Standards of AASL and AECT be a district goal? Or will local standards be developed?

3. What subject area standards have been or are being developed by the district?

4. How can these subject area standards (or in their absence, the curriculum) be analyzed to show the integration of the Information Literacy Standards for Student Learning? What process is to be used to determine where the information literacy skills will be integrated?

5. What plans can be made for the systematic integration of information literacy with the curriculum?

6. How will the integration of the information literacy skills be shown? For example, could a committee create a skills-by-grade matrix?

The Milton Hershey School took a different approach. Knowing the long-range goal of the school was to become standards- and performance-based, the library media specialists took the initiative and developed an initial plan for establishing information literacy skills. Their plan centered on developing five key objectives:

- A framework

- Benchmarks

- Instructional strategies

- Assessment to show student mastery

- A process to integrate the skills across subject area curricula

Administrators, teachers, library media specialists, and technology staff were involved in implementing the objectives.

After studying standards for information literacy and technology, the group developed four standards as the basis for the program: accessing knowledge, producing knowledge, presenting knowledge, and knowledge for society and the workplace. These became their framework. The next step was to analyze each of the four standards in terms of prerequisite skills and content and link these to benchmark levels of grades 5, 8, and 10. Skill levels were developed for each benchmark, which in turn led to a scope and sequence statement. Each benchmark described a different skill level that also had to relate to an aspect of the school's curriculum (Jones, Gardner & Zaenglein, 1998). As the library media specialists were developing the information literacy standards, they were careful to involve various staff members. They asked for feedback and input to ensure staff agreement and use of the standards.

Implementation

How will the concept of information literacy be disseminated to teachers, parents, and administrators and be integrated with other curricula? Again, there is no single method for doing this. A lot depends on what already exists at the school. In one school district where an information literacy curriculum already existed the library media specialists looked at the existing curricula, noted where certain skills were currently being taught, and then wrote the information literacy skills into those curricula. The library media specialists then provided training to teachers on what skills were being taught in each curriculum. An important part of the inservices was to assure teachers that the

Ossining High School Library

library media specialists would work with them in teaching the skills (Joie Taylor, personal experience, 2000).

Another example shows how a building level library media specialist integrated information literacy skills into a new technology curriculum. First, at a staff meeting she introduced the teachers to what she was going to do and had them complete a survey assessing their technology skills. Then she met with each teacher individually or by grade level. At the meeting the following issues were covered: 1) the new keyboarding curriculum for their grade level, 2) the current information literacy curriculum objectives they personally could integrate within their classroom setting, 3) which technology skill(s) they would personally like to improve upon during the next school year, 4) a listing of the integrated projects (information literacy and technology) already in place for their grade, and 5) in which areas they wished to integrate information literacy and technology during the next school year. Following the meetings with teachers, a schedule was drawn up of what teachers wanted done each month. This allowed the library media specialists to do advanced planning and help with scheduling classes (interview with Tongay Epp, April 10, 2003).

Farmer (1999) reported on how Redwood High School used information literacy to help students meet district outcomes. The starting point was the fact that students had difficulty in accessing and evaluating information. A study group made up of the library media specialist and teachers was formed to discuss issues, direct group work, and provide two-way communication. Then a "Research Strategies Skills Inventory" was developed as a method of assessing information literacy skills aligned with the standards in *Information Power: Building Partnerships for Learning*. Figure 4.1 is an example of such an inventory.

The faculty and students were then surveyed as to whether assignments incorporated those skills. The results of the survey were mapped and colored-coded by department.

After seeing the results of the survey, the faculty adapted the inventory and shared responsibility for incorporating the skills throughout the curriculum. A variety of methods were used to accomplish the incorporation, including redesigning assignments, adding instruction, incorporating technology, and varying presentation formats. In addition, rubrics for process and product and online teaching aids were developed.

Farmer's analysis of why the project was effective is a key element in planning for information literacy instruction. She felt that the project was effective because it grew out of a teacher-perceived need; the effort was student centered; classroom teachers and library media specialists were partners, both taking leadership responsibility for the product and the impact; and the entire faculty was involved and "owned the process." Cooperation is critical when it comes to developing information literacy skills.

Class _____ Unit _____ Date _____

Assignment _____

AASL & AECT INFORMATION LITERACY STANDARD	LOCAL INFORMATION LITERACY SKILL	USE OF SKILL IN ASSIGNMENT		
		Not use skill	Assume knew skill	Taught skill
1. Accesses information efficiently and effectively.	1. Develops the question or problem.			
	2. Analyzes the assignment to find the main idea.			
	3. Chooses the best resources.			
	4. Locates information resources.			
	5. Locates information within resources.			
2. Evaluates information critically and competently.	1. Skims and scans resource for key ideas.			
	2. Determines if the information answers the question.			
	3. Records pertinent information (takes notes).			
	4. Respects principles of intellectual freedom.			
3. Uses information accurately and creatively.	1. Applies information through critical thinking and problem solving.			
	2. Determines the audience.			
	3. Determines the sequence of the information, e.g. outlines, storyboards.			
	4. Prepares product or project.			
4. Pursues information related to personal interests.	1. Includes personal application, interests, or insights in work.			
	2. Method of presentation appropriate to audience.			

Figure 4.1. Research Skills Strategy Inventory.

Classroom teachers often include information literacy skills in learning activities but don't realize they are doing so. When working with teachers in a middle school, one library media specialist had the teachers think about projects they were currently doing in their classes. They then identified any information literacy skills that were a part of the projects. The teachers were surprised to learn that about half the information literacy skills were already being taught. When the skills being taught in each class were combined, there were actually few new information literacy skills that had to be added. A key point in the teachers' understanding of integrating information literacy skills was the fact that every teacher did not have to teach all the skills. Knowing that the information literacy skills were spread over several subject areas and classes made the task seem more manageable (Joie Taylor, personal experience, 2000).

Integration

Teachers must accept the idea that information literacy skills must be taught in all classes frequently. Students should practice using information literacy skills, as skills not practiced are eventually lost. In addition, students need to use the skills in a variety of settings and projects to help them transfer the skills to new situations.

The library media specialist plays a critical role in implementing information literacy skills integration by introducing teachers to the skills through formal inservice programs, informal planning sessions, and casual conversations. Library media specialists should talk to teachers about what information literacy skills students are to learn and what background lessons students need. Students learn new information more easily if it is linked to preexisting knowledge. Thinking through where students will look for information and how they will record and evaluate what they find are tasks the library media specialist should do and share with the classroom teacher.

Taking a leading role in providing inservice and being a change agent are not roles that library media specialists have accepted readily. Pickard (1999) found that the instructional role most library media specialists in Georgia felt they did to a large extent was providing access to materials through organization and classification that put materials, regardless of format, into a unified collection. Providing reference services and materials to individual students and teachers was another instructional role in which library media specialists excelled. Less frequently practiced activities were the library media specialist participating as an equal partner with the teacher in assessing students' achievements in a resource-based unit and explaining various styles of learning that account for individual differences among students.

Activities related to instructional design and consultation seldom took place. Pickard concluded that most activities engaged in by library media specialists were related to the warehousing (selecting, organizing for retrieval, and assisting students) aspect of instruction. From this research the conclusion might be drawn that library media specialists are a part of the problem in integrating information literacy skills with other curricula. If library media specialists do not see their role as designing and evaluating instructional experiences for students, teachers and administrators probably will not either.

Library media specialists are not entirely to blame. Administrators play an important role in the success of the library media program. "Whenever library media programs have been especially successful, there have been strong, informed, and active partnerships forged among the principal, the classroom teachers, and the library media personnel" (Jay & Jay, 1990). One thing administrators can do is to see that library media specialists are part of all curriculum teams. When library media specialists are involved at the beginning stages of developing curriculum, they can help other teachers see how and where information literacy skills fit. Involvement on curriculum teams also aids in including information literacy skills at all levels. Integration of information literacy skills should begin in kindergarten and continue through all grades and subjects.

Change does not take place easily or rapidly, usually occurring over a period of three to five years. Recognizing some of the aids and barriers to integration can help the library media specialist make the change. The aids and barriers to integration of information literacy skills can be summarized as follows:

Aids to integration of information literacy skills:

- The principal's expectations of a teaching role for the library media specialist and that information literacy skills will be integrated with other curricula.

- Involvement of teachers in development of information literacy skills so they see the connections and how the skills actually help student learning.

- Research to show the importance of information literacy skills; being able to cite some of the research from Alaska, Colorado, and other states.

- Adherence to state/district standards of instruction and learning and how information literacy skills can be used to help students reach state standards.

Barriers to integration of information literacy skills:

- Teachers' attitudes and beliefs that information literacy skills are an add-on and there is no time during the day to teach them.

- Time available for teachers and library media specialists to work together so that planning for integration of information literacy skills can take place.

- Lack of administrative support; teachers do not consider information literacy important.

- Educational practices such as teaching from the textbook or reliance on standardized tests.

The pressure of the principal's expectations and time for training are essential. If the principal does not value information literacy, the staff won't either. Both the teachers and the library media specialist are needed to make students life-long learners, which is the ultimate goal of information literacy. Collaboration of teachers and library media specialists in providing optimum teaching and learning environments is also essential to achieving information literacy skills implementation. The principal has to ensure that there is time for the teacher and library media specialist to collaborate. The principal sets the tone. If collaboration is expected, it will happen.

Curriculum Mapping

Curriculum mapping is an important component in planning for information literacy instruction. Curriculum mapping shows what is being taught, by whom, and when, and enables teachers to identify gaps and repetitions, target areas of integration, and match assessment with standards (Hughes-Hassell & Wheelock, 2001). Curriculum mapping should support teacher discussions about how to implement a curriculum aligned with standards and assessment (Barron, 2003, p. 50). An important component of curriculum mapping is to identify overlapping topics that, if corrected will foster greater curriculum cohesiveness.

In information literacy, curriculum mapping can be defined as the process of identifying what information literacy skills are taught, in which curriculum each skill is taught, when it is taught, what skills need to be integrated, and which information literacy skills are used to help students reach state and local standards. Another component is to identify which curricula have not been integrated with information literacy skills. Alignment with state and local standards and assessments must always be considered.

Steps in Curriculum Mapping

Curriculum mapping should be undertaken with the support of the principal and the involvement of classroom teachers and the library media specialist. Hughes-Hassell and Wheelock (2001) suggest that the first step in curriculum mapping is to read about it in such books as *Mapping the Big Picture: Integrating Curriculum and Assessment K–12* by Heidi Hays Jacobs (1997). The reading is necessary to give those involved a background and vocabulary for working with curriculum mapping. The next step is to identify what information is needed. The information literacy skills taught, the units in which they were taught, the grade levels, how much time each unit took, the calendar quarter, the level of instruction, teaching methods, resources used, and the evaluation must be identified (Eisenberg & Berkowitz, 1988). Any links to state standards or benchmarks should also be noted. Making the links between state standards and assessments and information literacy skills is critical because it helps show how library media specialists work with teachers to meet those standards. Furthermore, teachers see how library media specialists can help them teach a standard rather than information literacy being an add-on.

The third step in curriculum mapping is to collect the data. Curriculum mapping is likely to take more than one year. There are several ways to collect data. The library media specialist can begin by keeping a record for a year of the information literacy skills taught in each grade or subject area and with which teachers. A spreadsheet or database can be developed in which to enter the data. Using collaboration forms is another way of gathering the data. By using either of these methods, the library media specialist can identify the areas of greatest need and target those for development first. These areas can be developed while the process of curriculum mapping is being completed.

The goal is to find areas in which information literacy skills can be integrated. Frequently the library media specialist uses observations and asks questions of the teacher or students. For example, teachers who ask to display student work in the library media center might be a place to start. A number of students from the same class asking for resource material might be a clue that some information literacy skills could be integrated.

Another way to identify information literacy needs is for the library media specialist to look for those places in the curricula where several resources are used and the evaluation is done in the form of a report or product. Since most of these learning experiences are tied to a standard, this is a natural place to show how information literacy skills can help students meet the standard.

Ideally, classroom teachers should be involved in conducting the curriculum mapping. This will give them a sense of ownership and provide a more accurate picture of what is happening in the classroom. A form may be provided, and everyone should use the same form to make the compilation of data easier. The problem with using a form, however, is that not everyone will complete it and not everyone will interpret the questions in the same way. In this case the results would be of limited use. If curriculum mapping is done with the idea of identifying areas of overlap and gaps in all curricula, there may be stronger support for this activity.

Finally, the data are mapped, analyzed, and used. The mapping can take the form of graphs, charts, tables, or any other format that meets the need. The maps should be reviewed for gaps and repeats. Evidences of standard practices should be found as well as areas for potential interdisciplinary and cross-grade-level collaboration. Learning goals and skills that require students to use information literacy skills should be noted. If resources are a part of the curriculum map, the library media center and classroom resources should include technology. Finally, the appropriate assessment to demonstrate learning should be delineated (Hughes-Hassell & Wheelock, 2001, pp. 66–67).

Benefits to the Library Media Specialist

The process of curriculum mapping has the potential of benefiting the entire school. Since the focus here is on the library media program and information literacy skills, the benefits to the library media specialist are discussed. According to Hughes-Hassell & Wheelock, curriculum mapping enables the library media specialist to

- make connections between content learning and information literacy skills

- collaborate with teachers to integrate information literacy competencies throughout the teaching and learning process

- create and promote rationale for infusing information literacy standards into curricular and instructional policies

- recommend appropriate information resources to support information literacy and critical thinking throughout the curriculum. (2001, p. 66)

Having identified an area of need, the library media specialist must take the next step and approach the teacher about adding the information literacy component. Chapter 5 deals in more detail about how this might be done. Some teachers are going to be resistant, but others will be enthusiastic. Probably hardest to accept is that there are teachers who will refuse to work with the library media specialist.

Collection Mapping

Collection mapping is defined as a form of evaluation that provides a way to determine the quantity and quality of the materials available in school media centers and, thus, to know exactly what materials are available for students at any time (Harbour, 2002, p. 6). Hughes-Hassell & Wheelock (2001) state that collection mapping is a process used to collect, present, and organize information about the library media collection of resources. Collection mapping is important to curriculum mapping in that without adequate, appropriate resources there is little need to identify areas in which to integrate information literacy skills. Teachers and students will become easily discouraged if they do not have the resources needed to complete projects.

Despite the time it takes, collection mapping has several benefits. It

1. identifies areas of strength and weaknesses in the collection

2. provides evidence of how the collection supports the curriculum and meets academic and recreational needs of students

3. shows how the library media center budget is being spent

4. provides data to use to lobby for extra funding

5. shows how a weeding plan matches curriculum priorities and identifies outdated, worn out, inaccurate, or irrelevant resources (Hughes-Hassell & Wheelock, 2001).

In collection mapping the library media specialist wants to go beyond simply identifying the quantity and quality of resources available. The resources must be identified in some way by subject areas in order to determine what curricula are being supported and where additional materials are needed. As in curriculum mapping, the support of the principal is important, and discussions with classroom teachers are essential.

Harbour (2002) outlines three steps for collection mapping.

1. Count the total collection.

    There are a number of ways a collection may be counted. If the media center is automated, the task is fairly easy. Most automation software will generate a report containing the number of items in a collection. If the media center is not automated, the library media specialist may want to estimate the number of volumes. One way to do this is to count the number of shelves and multiply by the average number of books on a shelf. Another common method is to use the shelflist and assume 100 books per inch of cards.

    Although the collection as a whole must be examined, it is also necessary to break it down into various parts. These parts could be special collections, such as Spanish language books or myths and tall tales. Another way to examine the collection is by its use in supporting research in different curricula. For example, count biographies and history materials related to the study of American history or a unit of study within American history. An informal way of identifying where collection mapping might be needed is based on experience. While teaching a unit, write down those areas for which students have trouble finding information. Also, note any times when several students request resources on the same topic.

2. Compute the number of items per student.

This step is accomplished by simply dividing the number of materials by the number of students. The library media specialist will have to decide if the number of students will be the entire student body or just those students in the classes most likely to use the materials. Whichever number is chosen, the library media specialist must make it clear what method has been used.

At this point the age of the materials should also be accessed. Automation systems often generate this type of information as a report. Some automation software vendors offer this service either free or for a small fee. Recording the date of every third item is another way of estimating the age of a collection. Age of materials is especially critical in areas such as science, geography, and social sciences but should be considered in all areas. Over a period of time writing styles and clothing change, and materials simply need an up-to-date look. Knowing the age of materials might also help build a case for an increase in a budget.

3. Present the results.

A graph is often an effective way to show the number of items in a collection and the age of that collection. Entering the numbers into a spreadsheet allows one to manipulate and graph the data in a variety of ways. The graphs must be accompanied by a written brief. Harbour (2002) states that three elements must be included in the results: 1) a brief introduction, which includes a brief history and demographics of the school; 2) the size of the collection; and 3) the quality of the collection. Graphs, charts, and rating scales are useful for items 2 and 3. Any special services outside of what might be expected should be noted. A school that has the only preschool program in the district is an example.

Hughes-Hassell & Wheelock (2001) outline slightly different steps in collection mapping that expand on Harbour's steps to include access to online resources:

1. Collect data on the total collection.

2. Collect data on the access students and teachers have to technology at home and through the Internet.

3. Collect data on specific areas of the collection such as the Civil War and Native Americans—those that cross Dewey Decimal areas.

4. Create a collection map using bar graphs, diagrams, or pie charts.

5. Analyze data to see where the collection meets curriculum needs, to find areas that need weeding, identify technology needs, and establish budget priorities.

6. Create proposed collection maps that will compare curriculum units and topics and decide what areas of the collection will need to change over the next five years.

Curriculum mapping and collection mapping are not just exercises to increase the budget, worthy as that goal might be. Mapping is done to determine the strengths and weaknesses of the collection to support the teaching of information literacy skills as well as independent reading. By involving teachers and administrators in the process, mapping opens discussion of integration of information literacy skills.

Conclusion

Generally the library media specialist must initiate integration of information literacy skills into various curricula. The first step is gaining the support of the administration, for without that support little can be accomplished. Knowing the faculty is important in determining how to begin the integration process. In some schools integration will come one teacher at a time over a period of years. The key is to know with which teacher to start. Who will to take the risk? Avoid starting with the teachers who are the wait and see type. Those teachers will come on board after they see the value in information literacy skills. In other schools, because of special needs or curriculum revisions, integrating information literacy can become part of a formal process. Important to keep in mind is to start. Teachers usually don't come to the library media specialist unless they have had experience working with one. Starting small is still starting, and change will take place.

Curriculum mapping and collection mapping can be used to gain teacher support. As they work with the information literacy skills to integrate them in a variety of different curricula, teachers establish a sense of ownership in seeing that the skills are taught. Teachers begin to see how information literacy skills can help them as they work with students to meet state standards. Letting teachers have input into what resources are provided through the library media center is always a powerful incentive.

CHAPTER 5

Collaboration with a Purpose

Collaboration. Collaboration. Collaboration. Professional journals are full of the need for teachers to collaborate with each other to develop the best learning experiences for students. That need is no less important to library media specialists, who must work with all teachers. Studies in Oregon, Iowa, and New Mexico have found that successful group visits to the library media center depend on close collaboration between the library media specialist and teacher, planning and delivering the instruction together (Lance & Loertscher, 2003). Collaboration provides the framework for integrating information literacy skills with the other curricula of a school. Tschamler states that, "Because no one simply uses information skills without having a purpose or reason, collaboration provides an opportunity to create a purpose in conjunction with a lesson, in order to teach students the value of information and research skills" (2002, p. 14).

Information literacy skills must be taught at the point where students need them. Thus collaboration with classroom teachers is critical. Taught in isolation, information literacy skills are not retained by students because they see no need to learn the skill, nor do they get much immediate practice in using the skill. Taught in conjunction with what they are learning in the classroom, students are motivated to learn information literacy skills and are on their way to becoming independent thinkers and life-long learners. Not only is collaboration necessary, but implementation of flexible scheduling is also needed. (See Chapter 6 for more on flexible scheduling.)

Library media specialists must understand the effectiveness of collaboration and also be able to convey that understanding to teachers and administrators. A key point to remember is that collaboration requires shared goals and a shared vision, as well as a climate of trust between the library media specialist and the teacher. Principals, teachers, and library media specialists all must understand collaboration and team teaching. It is essential for these educators to rethink how they can work together.

49

Benefits of Collaboration

Through collaboration teachers and library media specialists are provided the opportunity to work together and share their expertise and knowledge Collaboration is meaningful and worthwhile only if there are strong benefits or outcomes. *Information Power* (AASL & AECT, 1998) states that the catalyst for collaboration is meeting the learning needs of students. Doiron and Davies (1998) identified five benefits of collaboration:

1. More effective use of resources. Resource-based learning requires more resources than can usually be provided in each classroom. Library media specialists spend time and effort carefully selecting resources that correlate with the curricula of the school and extend beyond the school to include community resources.

2. More effective use of teaching time. Two teachers working together share ideas and teaching responsibilities, and provide two teachers with whom students can work. The workload is divided, and teaching experience is doubled.

3. Integration of educational technologies. Library media specialists can help classroom teachers develop plans and ways to use computers and other technologies as teaching tools.

4. Shared efforts at promoting literacy. Together the teacher and library media specialist create an environment in which love of reading can flourish.

5. Developing the goal of life-long learning. Students are taught a research process that can be used throughout their lives. Using the process in different curricula helps students understand the transferability of the research process. In her research McGregor (2003) found that principals believed students became more independent users of the library media center with collaborative planning.

Loertscher and Achterman (2002) list these additional benefits of collaboration:

• Discipline problems are cut in half. Discipline problems are most likely lessened because students are engaged in what they are doing and because there are two teachers interacting with students. Another factor might be that students know they have to meet the same standards and consequences as the classroom, thus giving the library media specialist more credibility as a specialized teacher.

• There is more time to deal with individual student differences, abilities, learning styles, etc.

- Once again, with two teachers working with students, the ability to meet individual student needs increases.

- The teachers encourage each other when things get tough.

The School, Children, and Young People's Section of the Nebraska Library Association and the Nebraska Educational Media Association (2000) outline benefits for students when teachers and library media specialists do collaborative planning. One benefit that has been mentioned elsewhere is that information literacy skills are taught when needed, and therefore students see the skills as being relevant to their learning. In turn, the students see learning and reading as being relevant, and life-long learning skills are mastered. Other student befits include the following:

- Excitement about learning is inherent.

- Varied learning styles are met.

- The work of small groups and independent study are facilitated.

- Optimum use of a variety of resources is made possible.

As mentioned above, another benefit of collaboration is that students become independent users of libraries. Collaboration can also increase student achievement. This happens because library media specialists are involved with integrating, organizing, and demonstrating the context and use of various types of resources (Milbury, 2005). Reducing the incidences of plagiarism can result from collaboration as the library media specialist works with the classroom teacher to design assignments that require students to show evidence of critical thinking and synthesis of information (Milbury, 2005).

The Collaborative Planning Process

Collaborative planning is a process. To be effective, library media specialists and classroom teachers must work together on all aspects of the unit: planning, teaching, and evaluating. Two heads are better than one. During collaboration the teacher and library media specialist brainstorm, discuss, and lay out the activities of a unit. Each person brings to the planning process the ability and willingness to share ideas, resources, teaching, and evaluation roles, as well as an understanding of how to implement best practices to meet content knowledge standards (Callison, 2003a). Thomas (2002) suggests that there are six steps in the collaborative planning process.

Step 1:   Invitation to the Classroom Teacher

Many teachers do not have the experience of working with library media specialists collaboratively. Therefore, the library media specialist must take the initiative and approach the classroom teacher. There are several ways to raise teacher awareness of collaboration. Probably the most common and effective is simply to find a teacher who is open to collaboration and talk to that person about the possibility. Have a specific idea or example in mind. Another approach would be to issue an invitation in a newsletter or at a faculty meeting; however, keep in mind that follow-up will be necessary. Logan (2000) suggests additional ways to encourage collaboration:

- Listen for openings and offer to assist through materials or actual involvement.
- Anticipate research projects and offer services in teaching research skills. This might become more effective if the procedure of curriculum mapping were used.
- When asked to pull resources, express a willingness to do so, but suggest that students could develop their skills by assisting in locating materials.
- Develop note-taking strategies to share with teachers.
- Suggest, develop, or expand upon projects during conversations.
- Serve on curriculum committees.

A key factor here is building a trust relationship. Many teachers do not know that library media specialists can help them. Collaboration allows the library media specialist to showcase his or her collaboration skills (Milbury, 2005). Teachers have to sense that a library media specialist understands what is happening in the classroom, knows the curriculum, and cares about students. Building a sense of trust often takes two or three years, or even longer with some teachers.

Step 2:   Flexible Planning

Collaboration can be a formal session at which the classroom teacher and library media specialist sit down and plan, or it can be informal, using memos, hallway conferences, or e-mails. In the beginning a more formal session is desirable, with the teacher and media specialist setting aside a specific time to meet. Follow-up can be more informal. With experience the formal meeting time will become shorter. Meet with the teacher at his or her convenience, whether that is during planning time, before school, after school, or during lunch. Both the teacher and the library media specialist need a clear understanding of a unit's focus and goals. During the planning session the following should be addressed:

- Which goals and objectives will be taught in both the content area and the information literacy curriculum? What are the prerequisite skills?
- What instructional activities will be used to teach the objectives?
- Which step(s) of the research process will be emphasized or reviewed?
- What is the final project?
- What form of assessment will be used to measure the learning of the classroom content and the information literacy skills?
- Who does what?
- What is the timeline for the unit?
- What resources are needed?

Step 3: Stay Actively Involved

Both the classroom teacher and the library media specialist should be actively involved during all class sessions. Sometimes the library media specialist will teach an objective, and at other times the classroom teacher will. Both, however, are in the classroom or library media center monitoring and assisting students. A value in having the classroom teacher present is in helping students to make connections with previous learning experiences.

Step 4: Share Responsibilities

Both the teacher and the library media specialist should develop the necessary learning materials, teach the lessons, and evaluate the students.

Step 5: Reflect

Often overlooked, reflection is a critical step. Reflect on the collaboration process. Also, look for ways to improve the lesson. Make notes to be filed with the lesson plan for use in another year.

Step 6: Save the Lesson

Save the lesson, even if there is room for improvement. There is no need to start over every year; time is too precious. Build on what has been done.

Once a few teachers start collaborating, others will see the benefit and initiate a project. About 2.5 percent of teachers will be innovators and ready to start immediately. Some 12.5 percent of teachers are early adopters and are more cautious, taking longer to accept new ideas. The early majority, about 35 percent of the teachers, are the wait-and-see group. If the early adopters have success, the early majority will give a new idea a try. Another 35 percent are the late majority. They are difficult to influence and will adopt only when many others have. Last are the 15 percent who are resisters or laggards. They don't like change and will be the last to accept collaboration, if they ever do at all (Extra Edge, 1995). Remember that no matter how great the idea, change is a long process. Effective change takes three to five years. Also, remember that some teachers will never accept collaboration. Forget about them and concentrate on those who are willing collaborate. The library media specialist's responsibility is to see that the information literacy skills are taught. If one subject or grade has little collaboration, the deficiency will have to be made up elsewhere.

Roles in Collaboration

Collaboration involves an ongoing conversation between teachers and the library media specialist. They must come to understand their shared goals for student learning and each other's roles in the collaboration process. Both the classroom teachers and the library media specialist have specific areas of expertise they bring to the collaboration process. The classroom teacher knows the students' strengths and weaknesses, attitudes, and interests. Teachers are familiar with learning processes and teaching strategies that work best for their students. The content or objectives that must be taught are known by the classroom teacher. They are familiar with state standards and what must be assessed.

The library media specialist brings knowledge of resources, information literacy skills, and information processes to the collaborative process. Using the knowledge of student abilities and what is being taught in the classroom, library media specialists develop a collection that supports the curriculum. Knowledge of these resources is used to suggest appropriate materials for classroom learning experiences. The library media specialist knows what skills are needed to access information in various formats and can teach students those skills. Both the teacher and the library media specialist bring an understanding of teaching methods and a wide range of strategies. As Callison (2003a) states, the team of classroom teacher and library media specialist becomes a curricular think tank.

A more specific examination of the roles that the library media specialist and classroom teacher play, both separately and together, reveals that the library media specialist

- learns what is taught in the classroom and how information literacy skills can be integrated through curriculum mapping by teachers and through membership on the school's curriculum committee;

- knows the research process;

- knows how to integrate technology to enhance learning;

- knows available resources within the library media center (both print and electronic) and makes them available to all staff and students;

- knows resources available outside the library media center, both in the community and electronically;

- shares with teachers and administrators the advantages to students of a collaborative process;

- conducts inservices about both national and local information literacy standards;

- maintains records of skills and processes taught;

- meets, plans, and teaches with the classroom teacher; and

- adapts planning sessions to meet the different styles of classroom teachers.

The classroom teacher

- agrees to collaborate;

- has knowledge of the curriculum;

- knows the learning process;

- knows the current state standards or district curriculum;

- knows the students, including their learning styles, reading abilities, entry level abilities, and experiences as a group;

- knows teaching strategies;

- shares assignments with the library media specialist and discusses what students need in the way of information literacy skills;

- gives assignments that require higher order thinking skills; and

- meets, plans, and teaches with the library media specialist.

Together the library media specialist and classroom teacher

- design teaching and learning activities;

- have a repertoire of successful practices to draw upon;

- share teaching responsibilities;

- stimulate student thinking by asking questions;

- help students identify information needs;

- assist in the research process;

- evaluate use of learning resources, achievement of objectives, and products and processes;

- challenge assumptions and conclusions;

- identify and correct misconceptions;

- model thinking and encourage reflection;

- guide inquiry;

- question the probable findings;

- evaluate the unit; and

- keep current with research on learning behavior.

Students also have a role in collaboration, although it is very different from that of either the classroom teacher or the library media specialist. The role of the students is to obtain knowledge and understanding in order to meet the curricular objectives and standards. In order to do that the students bring to the collaboration

- enthusiasm for active learning and

- a sense of responsibility for meeting teacher expectations.

Barriers to Collaboration

Teachers proceed through a developmental sequence. Where they are on the developmental continuum may influence their ability and willingness to collaborate. According to Katz (1995), teachers advance through four developmental stages:

• Stage I—Survival. The teachers' main concern is whether or not they can survive the school year. This stage usually lasts one year but can continue into the second year of teaching. Teachers are seeking rules and recipes to guide their actions. At this stage teachers need support, understanding, encouragement, reassurance, comfort, and guidance.

• Stage II—Consolidation. At this stage teachers are ready to consolidate the overall gains made during the first stage and to differentiate specific tasks and skills to be mastered next. Teachers make conscious choices and are able to change lessons as they see the need. Suggestions for using a wider range of resources would be timely.

• Stage III—Renewal. During the third or fourth year of teaching teachers begin to tire of doing the same old thing. Students are flexibly grouped and regrouped as skills develop. New developments in the field are sought. New ways for teaching concepts are welcomed.

• Stage IV—Maturity. At the maturity stage teachers have reached a comfortable level of confidence concerning their competence. Some teachers reach this stage within three years, while others take five or more. Teachers easily manage classrooms and can anticipate problems. They are now ready to ask deeper and more abstract questions in order to increase student learning.

Library media specialists must be cognizant of a teacher's stage of professional development. Beginning teachers need a lot of support. Since they are usually eager for help, suggestions of ways to work together may be readily accepted. Keep in mind, however, that they usually have no experience with or a model for collaboration and will need to be led through the process. At the consolidation stage, build on any collaborative efforts that have been established. If the idea of collaboration is new, provide resources along with suggestions of how teachers might use them. Teachers at the renewal stage are ready for a change. These are the teachers who will most likely welcome collaboration. Seek them out when first beginning the collaboration process in a school. Mature teachers may be harder to convince, as they are comfortable with what they are doing. Through inservice and research studies, show them how collaboration makes a difference to the students.

A teacher's stage of professional development is not the only barrier. As was discovered by the Library Power Project, "collaboration was more difficult when, despite the librarian's efforts, teachers persisted in viewing the library as a service to support traditional instruction rather than a resource for instructional change" (*Findings*, 1999, p. 16). If this attitude is common, the library media specialist must volunteer for school committees, join curriculum teams, and present inservices to show the benefits of collaboration.

Leonard and Leonard (2003) found that lack of time is an important teacher concern about collaboration. Teachers mentioned other school activities, such as parent conferences, programs, activities, and committee work. The everyday activities of planning lessons, helping children who were absent or needing extra help, and grading papers were also mentioned. Leaving right after school for a second job was another time-related factor. Indirectly related to the time issue is the fact that lunch periods and planning times do not always coincide with when the library media specialist is available.

Another barrier that Leonard and Leonard (2003) reported were teachers not wanting to stay after school, especially if they were not being paid. Two other barriers were teacher personality conflicts and lack of administrative support. Without administrative support, collaboration is almost impossible, except with a few teachers.

Aids to Collaboration

No single factor can be said to ensure effective collaboration. Instead, there are several factors that help facilitate collaboration. "Collaborative planning is impacted by the individuals involved, school climate, time for planning, the organization of the school, the facility and collection and training; of these, the characteristics and actions of the people involved are most important" (Haycock, 1999).

One factor is the principal's expectations. Van Deusen and Tallman (1994) found that more consultation or collaboration took place when principals expected team planning. Consequently, the library media specialist must forge a partnership with the principal that includes a shared vision for the library media program encompassing collaboration and flexible scheduling. A study completed in Pennsylvania found that activities helpful in integrating information literacy with other curricula were teaching cooperatively with teachers as well as teaching alone, providing inservice training to teachers, serving on standards and curriculum committees, and managing information technology (Lance & Loertscher, 2003, p. 4). A supportive principal can be instrumental in seeing that some of these activities take place.

Another important factor is flexible scheduling. When the library media specialist is scheduled for a whole day of classes, coming at the same time each week, there is little time for collaboration. This type of schedule restricts teacher access to the library media specialist. In addition, there is little time available to teach information literacy skills in a manner conducive to student learning. In other words, with a fixed schedule students do not have access to the library media center or the library media specialist several days in a row during the times classes meet.

Flexible scheduling allows the classroom teacher and the library media specialist to plan the amount of time that is needed for students to complete resource-based projects and other learning activities. If need be, classes can be scheduled to use the library media center and receive instruction on use of resources for several consecutive days. Without this concentrated block of time, research projects drag on and on, resulting in lower student enthusiasm for learning. Flexible scheduling is discussed in more depth in Chapter 6.

Adequate staffing is also a factor. *Information Power: Guidelines for School Library Media Programs* (AASL & AECT, 1988) recommends at least one full-time library media specialist in every library media center. When the student population reaches 1,000, another library media specialist should be added. In their research Lance, Welborn and Hamilton-Pennell (1993) found that the size of a library media center's staff and collection is the best school predictor of academic achievement. In a second study Lance, Rodney and Hamilton-Pennell (2000) found that elementary and middle schools students did better on tests when the school library media specialist and classroom teacher collaborated. The research indicates that staff and collaboration influence student achievement. Reading scores increased 8 to 21 percent (Lance & Loertscher, 2003). Yet school decision makers continue to staff library media centers with clerks and technicians, resulting in the library media center being nothing more than a warehouse of books.

In order to carry out collaboration, time to plan is critical. "Collaboration was most effective when teachers had already done some planning specifically aimed at improving learning objectives or thematic units" (*Findings,* 1999, p. 16). Therefore, not only do teachers need time to plan and think ahead; they also need time to plan with the library media specialist. Without good planning, little is accomplished. Time is needed for the partners to decide on goals, discuss learning activities, and develop assessments. Without adequate time to plan, collaboration cannot be carried out.

Many library media specialists find using a collaboration form or planning guide helpful. Figure 5.1 (p. 60) is an example of a collaboration form. All such forms have certain characteristics. They include information about the class level and size, a timeline, the teacher's name, the information literacy skill to be taught, the content objective to be taught, the state standard, the responsibilities of the teacher and library media specialist, the student project, how the learning will be assessed, the materials or resources needed, and a space for comments or evaluation of the unit.

Teacher's Name: _____ Grade: _____ Today's Date: _____
Unit: _____ No. Students: _____

Timeline: _____ Dates of class: _____ Time of class: _____

State Standards:	Information Literacy Standards:

Classroom Objectives:	Information Literacy Objectives:

Learning activities: Resources needed:	Who will do:

Evaluation of Unit:

Figure 5.1. Collaboration Form.

A checklist of information literacy skills to be taught at each grade level is also helpful. The checklist will help ensure that students are taught the required skills. The list can also be used to share with teachers what the library media specialist is expected to teach, thus opening the possibility of collaboration. Figure 5.2 (pp. 62–64) is an example of such a checklist, maintained in a spreadsheet. The first column refers to the research step. In this case the appropriate Big6™ step. The second column is the information literacy skill. The third column indicates whether the skill is to be introduced, practiced, or mastered. The date the skill is taught is entered in the fourth column. The fifth column is the class. In the activities/comments column is placed information regarding in which unit the skill was taught and any other information the library media specialist wants to remember for future use.

One library media specialist has used the list of information literacy objectives to further collaboration. After having worked with the teachers for a year and noting when and how each of the objectives was taught, the library media specialist met with teachers at each grade level. Teachers were given a copy of what was to be taught at their grade level as well as what was taught the previous year. Each objective was written on a slip of paper. Knowing that teachers include some information literacy skills within the classroom, the teachers were asked to identify any that they taught. For example, the fourth-grade teachers used a thesaurus. A notation was made beside that information literacy objective indicating that the classroom teacher covered that concept. The teachers and library media specialist then brainstormed how the other objectives could be met while at the same time helping teachers with meeting state curriculum standards (Joie Taylor, personal experience, 2003).

McGriff, Harvey, and Preddy (2004) suggest that library media specialists need to collect quantitative and qualitative data to analyze collaboration triumphs and productivity. They suggest using semester surveys, collaboration logs, student surveys, and collaborator-educator surveys to collect data. Quantitative data are numerical responses that can easily be put into a spreadsheet for quick interpretation. Qualitative data are collected using open-ended questions and personal comments or experiences. A semester survey could be given to faculty, administration, and support staff. Questions should relate to curriculum and services. A numerical scale would be developed representing terms such as Never used, Frequently used, or Used once a year. How many numbers used and the terms used will obviously depend on what information is being collected. Examples of questions for a semester survey are:

What resources were not available to your or your students that the library media center should consider adding?

What could be done to improve the service of the library media center?

What barriers are there to using the library media center?

Big6™	Information Literacy Objective	Level	Date	Class	Activity/Comments
1TD	Initiates own questions on topics	Intro	3/3	5C	5H ocean project
1TD	Initiates own questions on topics	Intro	3/3	5H	5H ocean project
1TD	Initiates own questions on topics	Intro	3/3	5P	5H ocean project
2ISS	No one source contains all points of view or all info available on topic	P	3/4	5C	5H ocean project
2ISS	No one source contains all points of view or all info available on topic	P	3/4	5H	5H ocean project
2ISS	No one source contains all points of view or all info available on topic	P	3/4	5P	5H ocean project
4UofI	Explain plagiarism and avoid its use	P	3/3	5C	5H ocean project
4UofI	Explain plagiarism and avoid its use	P	3/3	5H	5H ocean project
4UofI	Explain plagiarism and avoid its use	P	3/3	5P	5H ocean project
4UofI	Record bibliographic info: author, title, copyright	P	3/3	5C	Ocean project
4UofI	Record bibliographic info: author, title, copyright	P	3/3	5H	Ocean project
4UofI	Record bibliographic info: author, title, copyright	P	3/3	5P	Ocean project
4UofI	Record bibliographic info: author, title, copyright	P	10/16	5C	Native Americans
4UofI	Record bibliographic info: author, title, copyright	P	10/16	5H	Native Americans
4UofI	Record bibliographic info: author, title, copyright	P	10/16	5P	Native Americans
4UofI	Record pertinent info by note taking, charting, graphical aids, highlighting, etc.	P	10/16	5C	Native Americans— webbing
4UofI	Record pertinent info by note taking, charting, graphical aids, highlighting, etc.	P	10/16	5H	Native Americans—webbing

4UofI	Record pertinent info by note taking, charting, graphical aids, highlighting, etc.	P	10/16	5P	Native Americans—webbing
5Syn	Cite bibliographic information with product	P	3/10	5C	Ocean project
5Syn	Cite bibliographic information with product	P	10/21	5C	Native Americans
5Syn	Cite bibliographic information with product	P	3/10	5H	Ocean project
5Syn	Cite bibliographic information with product	P	10/21	5H	Native Americans
5Syn	Cite bibliographic information with product	P	3/10	5P	Ocean project
5Syn	Cite bibliographic information with product	P	10/21	5P	Native Americans
5Syn	Organize the presentation	P	10/23	5C	Native Americans-what makes good poster
5Syn	Organize the presentation	P	10/23	5H	Native Americans-what makes good poster
5Syn	Organize the presentation	P	10/22	5P	Native Americans-what makes good poster
5Syn	Prepare for presentation (how to give)	P	3/18	5C	Mr Hameister did in class-Ocean project
5Syn	Prepare for presentation (how to give)	P	3/18	5H	Hameister did in class-Ocean project
5Syn	Prepare for presentation (how to give)	P	3/18	5P	Hameister did in class-Ocean project
5Syn	Present product	P	10/31	5C	Native Americans

Figure 5.2. Information Skills Taught—Fifth Grade. Form used by Columbus (NE) Public Schools (Columbus, 1998). *(Cont. on p. 64)*

5Syn	Present product	P	10/31	5H	Native Americans
5Syn	Present product	P	10/31	5P	Native Americans
6Eval	Decide what improvement for future (product)	P	10/31	5C	Native Americans, Cuba did
6Eval	Decide what improvement for future (product)	P	10/31	5P	Native Americans, Cuba did
6Eval	Determine strengths & weaknesses of research process & product	P	10/31	5C	Ms Cuba did evaluation of presentation in class.
6Eval	Determine strengths & weaknesses of research process & product	P	10/31	5H	Ms Cuba did evaluation of presentation in class.
6Eval	Determine strengths & weaknesses of research process & product	P	10/31	5P	Ms Cuba did evaluation of presentation in class.
6Eval	Decide what improvement for future (product)	P	10/31	5P	Native Americans, Cuba did

Key:

Column 1: The number refers to the Columbus Public Schools goal.

TD = Task Definition

ISS = Information Seeking Strategies

U of I = Use of Information

Syn = Synthesis

Eval = Evaluation

Column 5: Class

The numbers and letters refer to the grade and teacher, for example, 5H is Mr. Hameister's fifth-grade class.

Figure 5.2. (Continued)

Evidence need not be limited to surveys. Collaboration forms can be used to create a collaboration log showing how often collaboration is done, with which teachers, and in what subject areas it was completed. A summary of the collaborative learning lessons should be developed. Although only effective learning experiences are included in the log, if the collaboration form includes an evaluation element, some examples of what went well and what resources are needed has already been provided. In order to document positive interactions with faculty and to show that some teachers recognize the value of collaboration, the library media specialist may also want to include e-mail such as this example:

> Have you ever done an American Revolution project? I did not know what kind of resources we have available in the library. I was thinking a small research project about a person, event, battle etc. Maybe include illustrations about topic??? We could even do the first part of research in the library and finish in the classroom or do something in the computer lab??? I would be looking at approximately the 2nd of February if all goes as planned, but I am flexible?? What do you think? Any ideas??? (Brenda Cuba, personal communication, January 17, 2005)

McGriff, Harvey, and Preddy (2004) explain that the collaboration log is used to record information as instructional units are planned. The collaboration form in Figure 5.1 (p. 60) or any of several others can be used for this purpose. The information obtained from the collaboration form helps the library media specialist determine who is and is not being served and what instructional needs are being met. The checklist in Figure 5.2 is another way that the library media specialist can easily ascertain the status of instruction.

The student survey is a part of evaluation data. Students are asked to respond to quantitative and qualitative questions in order to gather information about their experiences. Questions could be asked about how clear both the teacher's and the library media specialist's instructions were, if there were sufficient resources, and what they might do better or differently next time. An important part of this evaluation, according to McGriff, Harvey, and Preddy (2004), is for the teacher and library media specialist to discuss the responses together. Through this final process the collaborator-educator survey is compiled.

Conclusion

Some teachers embrace collaboration right away, while others take a wait-and-see attitude and jump on the bandwagon only after they see the positive effects of collaboration. There are other teachers who never accept collaboration. Rather than telling teachers what will be done, give them options for how to proceed with collaboration. Think of teachers as being at various stages along a continuum of collaboration. On one end is independence and on the other interdependence. At the beginning participants in collaboration must share their stories and look for new ideas together. As teachers and library media specialists progress along the continuum, they move on to giving aid and assistance to each other and then mutual sharing. Only when a degree of trust has been established and tested will the partners enter joint work or interdependence (Herrin, 1994). Toni Buzzeo (2002) states that the keys to successful collaboration include

- respecting individual strengths;

- advertising successes and building on them;

- remaining flexible; everyone will not participate at the same level;

- learning to compromise in order to move forward;

- remembering that word of mouth is the best form of advertising; and

- keeping the faith; collaboration works.

A colleague is fond of saying, "Baby steps. Take baby steps" (Jane Dodson, personal communication, 2003). Start with several small steps, one at a time, and move forward. Change takes years to accomplish, but it can be done.

CHAPTER 6

Flexible Scheduling

Scheduling is frequently discussed when media specialists get together. A question often asked is, "Do you have flexible scheduling?" What follows is usually dialog about fixed scheduling and the need to provide teacher planning time and whether there are ways to change that. *Information Power: Guidelines for Building Partnerships* (AASL & AECT, 1988) brought to the attention of library media specialists the benefits of flexible scheduling for the library media program to meet the needs of the school community. Both the library media center and the library media specialist's time can be flexibly scheduled. The focus of this chapter is scheduling the library media specialist's time in order to teach information literacy skills.

Types of Scheduling

According to Karpisek (1989, p. 41), scheduling serves 1) to ensure equitable access, 2) to help the library media specialist know what to plan in order to teach information literacy skills, and 3) to help the specialist assess library media center use. There are generally three types of scheduling: fixed, flexible, and a modified flexible schedule. Issues of fixed versus flexible schedules are mostly a concern at the elementary level. High schools and middle schools generally have a fixed length of period, 45 minutes for example, for each class, and classes are scheduled at specific times on specific days. The use of the library media center is often confined to those times. The only flexibility is how many days the center will be needed. Elementary schools are not as rigidly scheduled, and teachers have more latitude in scheduling classes.

Fixed Schedules

On a fixed schedule the library media specialist meets with each class on a specified day for a specified length of time all year long. Students are admitted to the media center only with a class or before and after school. The information literacy skills being taught often have little connection to what is being done in the classroom and therefore no relevance to the curriculum. The idea is that "library media" is another class just like music, art, and physical education (Karpisek, 1989). The justification that media specialists give for maintaining this type of schedule is that it ensures that every child is taught all the skills, but it is the least responsive to student and teacher needs.

Unfortunately, a fixed schedule is often used to provide planning time for classroom teachers; therefore, teacher involvement in what the students are learning is minimal. Library media specialists who must provide planning time for other teachers have little flexibility in when they teach skills. Information literacy skills are taught in the "it's the third week of September and time to teach about the encyclopedia" syndrome. There is no apparent concern about whether or not students need to use the encyclopedia at that time. Without teacher involvement and little or no connection to what is being learned in the classroom, students may not be learning the skills being taught.

Flexible Schedules

Flexible scheduling is one component of the larger concept of flexible access, open access being the second component. Both are needed to ensure that students and teachers have access to resources in a timely manner. Open access means that students come to the library media center whenever there is a need. Open access is what allows students to have adequate access to the library media center even when they are not scheduled for regular classes. The student need not be coming for a class but may be coming to check out a book, find the answer to a question, or do some recreational reading. Open access accommodates students of different ages levels and grades at the same time and in different groupings. Those grouping could be individuals, small groups, or classes.

What is a flexible schedule? Simply put, flexible scheduling means the schedule changes daily, weekly, and monthly. Teachers schedule classes according to project and unit needs (Karpisek, 1989). Changes in scheduling are necessitated by the fact that different students need to use the library media center on different days and for different lengths of time. When applied to instruction, a flexible schedule is critical if students are to be taught information literacy skills at the point of need. The library media specialist and the classroom teacher work together to determine the best time for instruction to occur. Who teaches the skills is also flexible. The instruction could be done by the library media specialist, the classroom teacher, or both.

A flexible schedule is also important to the integration of the information literacy curriculum with other curricular areas. The classroom teacher and the library media specialist determine at what points in the curriculum specific information literacy skills can be taught. Skills should be taught in different curricula for two reasons. First, students are more likely to remember information that connects with preexisting knowledge (Hardiman, 2003). Second, teaching in different subject areas is important for learning to transfer the skills from one setting to another. Using knowledge in multiple contexts helps students abstract relevant features of concepts and develop a more flexible representation of knowledge (Bransford, 2000). Since classes are taught at different times during the day and units are taught at different times of the year, the library media specialist must be available to teach the information literacy skills when students need them.

Advantages of Flexible Scheduling

There are several advantages for students and teachers when flexible scheduling is used. Those listed below relate to information literacy instruction.

- It is student centered.

- Students become better consumers of information through more frequent practice.

- Curricular needs are met.

- There is a lower student–teacher ratio.

One of the often overlooked advantages is the benefit to students. When the library media specialist's time is flexibly scheduled, students are the focus rather than the staff or planning time. Scheduling is done to optimize student learning. Students work on skills in a continuous manner rather than one day a week. They see a purpose for learning information literacy skills as they relate them to what they are learning in the classroom. Students are more motivated and excited about learning, as they know they need these skills to complete assignments (McGregor, 1999). Since they are allowed to use the library media center when they need to, students learn and practice information literacy skills when they are relevant. Also, students develop confidence in using libraries through successful experiences. Results from the Library Power Project indicate that students experienced more engaging and educationally rich learning activities when taught information literacy skills in context with classroom content (Library Power project, 2003).

Flexible scheduling promotes student use of information. Since students have ready access to the library media center, they use it more and for a wider variety of purposes. There are more opportunities to use the acquired information literacy skills. As students use the library media center more often and more independently, they become better information consumers. Being better consumers, the students can find information more efficiently, evaluate it with more care, and think critically about the content.

Another advantage is the focus on the curricula, both the information literacy curriculum and that being taught in the classroom. In the collaborative process the focus is on integrating the information literacy skills with the classroom objectives, thus dovetailing students' learning activities. The guiding factor is the teaching unit, not the time of the year or day of the week. If a unit takes 50 minutes a day for two weeks, that can be scheduled. If only one 45-minute period is needed, that is what is scheduled. Collaborative planning is facilitated by flexible scheduling. McGregor (2003) found that principals felt flexible scheduling provided better opportunities for collaboration as well as curriculum support. Van Deusen and Tallman (1994) found that more consultation occurred between teachers and library media specialists in schools with flexible scheduling. "Collaboration with colleagues and varied student use is more evident in schools with flexibly scheduled library resource centers" (Haycock, 1999). Knowing how to collaborate cannot be assumed. Haycock (1996) found that library media specialists who were trained in cooperative planning and teaching engaged in more collaboration than those who were not. If teachers don't know how to collaborate, the need for flexible scheduling is not as evident.

With flexible scheduling students also benefit by a lower student–teacher ratio. With both the library media specialist and the classroom teacher available to respond to students' questions, wait time for help is diminished, and students can stay on task more often. For high demand projects the library media para-educator can also assist students, thus further reducing the student–teacher ratio.

Challenges of Flexible Scheduling

Change is scary, and teachers and principals have some very real concerns about changing scheduling modes, including the following:

- **Providing planning time for other teachers.** In some schools the specialists (music, physical education, computer, library media) provide planning time for teachers. With flexible scheduling the library media specialist must be available to schedule classes as they are needed, thus preventing them from being available at the same time every week to provide planning time. Teachers need planning time, principals need to find a way to provide it, and to lose the use of the library media specialist's time as one avenue to providing planning time is threatening.

- **Changing existing educational activities.** Teachers have different personalities. Some welcome suggestions; others do not. If flexible scheduling is to work, the library media specialist must often take the initiative in approaching the teacher. Some teachers find changing their classroom activities uncomfortable or even threatening.

- **Finding time to schedule the library media specialist.** Teachers are very busy, and some see collaborating with the library media specialist in providing flexible scheduling as just one more thing to do. As teachers become more accustomed to flexible scheduling, the problem is more the library media specialist having trouble finding time to work with them.

- **Making sure information literacy skills are taught.** Because of the need to meet state standards, both principals and teachers are concerned that students be taught the appropriate information literacy skills. If students do not have regularly scheduled library classes, how can teachers be sure they have learned the necessary skills? A library media specialist usually has a method to track what skills have been taught, when, and to whom.

Implementing a flexible schedule is not always easy. In moving to a flexible schedule, library media specialists are often working against well-entrenched attitudes of teachers and principals. McGregor (1999) found that the qualities of the library media specialist seemed to be a factor in successful implementation. Library media specialists should be flexible, energetic, have a sharing and facilitating mindset, be competent, be persistent, have an awareness of national trends and best practices, have a sense of humor, be enthusiastic, and have the ability to deal with a variety of people.

According to McGregor (2003), principals stated that with flexible scheduling 1) the library media specialist and teachers tend to be overextended due to high demand and 2) not all students use the library media center often enough. While the possibility is there for both of these problems to happen, that need not be the case. Flexible scheduling does not mean unscheduled or unplanned. Posting a schedule helps both the library media specialist and the teacher when scheduling time for instruction in information literacy skills. Both can see what times are available at a glance. If curriculum mapping has been done, the library media specialist has an idea of when units will need to be scheduled and can pencil those in and work around them. A good para-educator can alleviate some of the problem because this person not only checks books in and out, but can also help with reading guidance, take care of reading promotions, and assist in some of the instructional activities. With a para-educator performing clerical tasks and working under the supervision of the library media specialist on other activities, the library media specialist has more time to work with students and teachers. The library media specialist is busy because flexible scheduling works, and support staff is a critical element in that success.

Students learn to use and do use the media center independently. When they are comfortable finding needed materials, students do not hesitate to use the library media center. In addition, the center is available for classes and groups of various sizes. No longer must students wait until the entire class is scheduled for the media center. Provided the library media center is large enough and arranged appropriately, students are free to visit even when there is a class scheduled.

Flexible scheduling does require organization. A busy library media specialist cannot keep track of a changing schedule without some type of calendar. One library media specialist has a laminated piece of oak tag with 20 squares on it; 5 squares across (one for each day of the week) and 4 rows down, so that a total of 4 weeks can be scheduled at one time (see Figure 6.1).

At the beginning of each row is written the date of the first day of the week. As classes are scheduled, they are written on the schedule. Teachers have learned to check the schedule for open times. A color code is used to identify the type of activities on the schedule. Red entries are for scheduled classes, black is for times the library media specialist must do recess supervision, and green is for other meetings the library media specialist must attend, such as staff meetings and district meetings (Joie Taylor, personal experience, 2003). The color code is for the benefit of the library media specialist rather than the teachers. The teachers just want to know when the media specialist is available.

As a means of comparison, a fixed and a modified schedule are presented in Figures 6.2 (pp. 74–75) and 6.3 (pp. 76–77). There are library media specialists who feel that a modified or fixed schedule is better because it ensures every child has an opportunity to use the library media center. However, once teachers and administrators see the benefits of flexible scheduling for teaching information literacy skills, they usually find other ways to make sure students are able to check out books. Ignoring when and where students need to learn a particular skill flies in the face of what is known about how humans learn. A fixed schedule provides little time for needed collaboration between the teachers and the library media specialist. In the flexible schedule the library media specialists has several opportunities to see teachers during the day as well as during lunch and after school. Some library media specialists see a modified schedule as a compromise. In a modified schedule, some classes come at fixed times. Because younger students need more structure, a case might be made for scheduling preschool and kindergarten students at the same time every week. Certain days are left open to allow for classes to come multiple times during the week if necessary.

Week of	Monday	Tuesday	Wednesday	Thursday	Friday
April 5	8:15-9:00 1B-Sea Animals 10:45-11:30 3T What makes good poster 1:00-1:30 1B-Henkes	9:15-10:00 3U work on posters 10:45-11:30 3T work on posters 12:05-12:20 recess 1:00-1:40 2G-Parish 2:00-2:30 2L-Howe	9:50-9:20 KAE-Seuss 9:20-10:40 KAD-Seuss 12:00-12:30 1W-Crews 2:05-2:30 KPE-Seuss 2:30-2:55 KPD-Seuss 3:05 After school supervision	9:15-10:15 3U Presentation on famous people 10:15-11:00 3T Presentation on famous people 12:15-12:40 1E-Bunting 1:15-1:45 2K-Kline	No School
April 12	No School	12:05-12:20 recess 3:05 Staff meeting	12:30-1:15 3H 6 students Famous People- Note taking	12:30-1:15 3H Finish note taking, make bib	
April 19	12:30-1:15 3H What makes good poster 1:15-1:45 5P Game to review definitions of types of lit	12:05-12:20 recess 12:30-1:15 3H Finish poster, practice presentation 3:30 LMS W Park		2:15-2:55 5H Game to review definitions of types of lit	3:05 After school supervision 3:45 After School Program-Lab
April 26	9:30-12:00 3 classes 4V Research on states—note taking 1:15-1:45 5P Game to review definitions of types of lit	9:30-12:00 3 classes 4V Research on states—bib 12:05-12:20 recess 3:05 staff meeting	9:30-12:00 3 classes 4V Research on states 12:00 Early release day		9:30-12:00 3 classes 4V Demo Word to make brochure

Figure 6.1. Sample Flexible Schedule.

Key: The word letter combinations such as 1B, 2G, 2L,3H, 3U, 5P, 4V, 5P, and 5H refer to the grade and teacher. For example, 1B is first grade, Mrs. Briese; 2G is second grade, Mrs. Gassen. KAE and KPD refer to the kindergarten classes: KAE is kindergarten, morning, Mrs. Emerson; KPD is kindergarten, afternoon, Mrs. Duranski.

Week of	Monday	Tuesday	Wednesday	Thursday	Friday
April 5	8:15-8:45 Kdg Eme 8:45-9:15 Kdg -Dur 9:15-10:15 3 U work on Posters 10:15-10:45 3 T making poster 10:45-11:15 11:30-12:00 Lunch 12:00-12:30 Plan 12:30-1:00 2L Howe 1:00-1:30 2G Parish 1:30-2:00 2K Kline 2:00-2:30 Kdg-Eme 2:30-2:55 Kdg-Dur	8:15-8:45 4V 8:45-9:15 4MH 9:15-10:45 4CH 10:45-11:15 5C 11:15-11:45 5P 11:30-12:00 Lunch 12:05-12:20 Recess 12:30-1:00 5H 1:00-1:30 1W 1:30-2:00 1E 2:00-2:30 1B sea animals	8:15-8:45 Kdg Eme 8:45-9:15 Kdg -Dur 9:15-10:15 3 U work on Posters 10:15-10:45 3 T making poster 10:45-11:15 11:30-12:00 Lunch 12:00-12:30 Plan 12:30-1:00 2L Howe 1:00-1:30 2G Parish 1:30-2:00 2K Kline 2:00-2:30 Kdg-Eme 2:30-2:55 Kdg-Dur 3:05 After school superervision	8:15-8:45 4V 8:45-9:15 4MH 9:15-10:45 4CH 10:45-11:15 5C 11:15-11:45 5P 11:30-12:00 Lunch 12:05-12:20 12:30-1:00 5H 1:00-1:30 1W Crews 1:30-2:00 1E Bunting 2:00-2:30 1B sea animals 2:30-3:00	No School
April 12	No School	8:15-8:45 4V 8:45-9:15 4MH 9:15-10:45 4CH 10:45-11:15 5C 11:15-11:45 5P 11:30-12:00 Lunch 12:05-12:20 recess 12:30-1:00 5H 1:00-1:30 1W Crews 1:30-2:00 1E Bunting 2:00-2:30 1B Henkes 2:30-3:00 3:05 Staff meeting	8:15-8:45 Kdg- Eme 8:45-9:15 Kdg -Dur 9:15-10:15 3 U Present posters 10:15-10:45 3T work on posters 10:45-11:15 3H Note 11:30-12:00 Lunch 12:00-12:30 Plan 12:30-1:00 2L 1:00-1:30 2G 1:30-2:00 2K 2:00-2:30 Kdg-Eme 2:30-2:55 Kdg-Dur	8:15-8:45 4V 8:45-9:15 4MH 9:15-10:45 4CH 10:45-11:15 5C 11:15-11:45 5P 11:30-12:00 Lunch 12:05-12:20 12:30-1:00 5H 1:00-1:30 1W 1:30-2:00 1E 2:00-2:30 1B Henkes 2:30-3:00	

April 19	8:15-8:45 Kdg- Eme 8:45-9:15 Kdg -Dur 9:15-10:15 3 U Present posters 10:15-10:45 3T present posters 10:45-11:15 3H Note 11:30-12:00 Lunch 12:00-12:30 Plan 12:30-1:00 2L 1:00-1:30 2G 1:30-2:00 2K 2:00-2:30 Kdg-Eme 2:30-2:55 Kdg-Dur	8:15-8:45 4V 8:45-9:15 4MH 9:15-10:45 4CH 10:45-11:15 5C 11:15-11:45 5P 11:30-12:00 Lunch 12:05-12:20 recess 12:30-1:00 5H 1:00-1:30 1W 1:30-2:00 1E 2:00-2:30 1B 3:30 LMS W Park	8:15-8:45 Kdg- Eme 8:45-9:15 Kdg -Dur 9:15-10:15 3 U 10:15-10:45 3T present posters 10:45-11:15 3H Note 11:30-12:00 Lunch 12:00-12:30 Plan 12:30-1:00 2L 1:00-1:30 2G 1:30-2:00 2K 2:00-2:30 Kdg-Eme 2:30-2:55 Kdg-Dur	8:15-8:45 4V 8:45-9:15 4MH 9:15-10:45 4CH 10:45-11:15 5C 11:15-11:45 5P 11:30-12:00 Lunch 12:05-12:20 12:30-1:00 5H Game-literature 1:00-1:30 1W 1:30-2:00 1E 2:00-2:30 1B 2:30-3:00	3:05 After school supervision 3:45 After school program—Lab
April 26	8:15-8:45 Kdg- Eme 8:45-9:15 Kdg -Dur 9:15-10:15 3 U Present posters 10:15-10:45 3T Make posters 10:45-11:15 3H Note 11:30-12:00 Lunch 12:00-12:30 Plan 12:30-1:00 2L 1:00-1:30 2G 1:30-2:00 2K 2:00-2:30 Kdg-Eme 2:30-2:55 Kdg-Dur	8:15-8:45 4V Note taking states 8:45-9:15 4MH 9:15-10:45 4CH 10:45-11:15 5C 11:15-11:45 5P Games-Literature 11:30-12:00 Lunch 12:05-12:20 recess 12:30-1:00 5H 1:00-1:30 1W 1:30-2:00 1E 2:00-2:30 1B 3:05 staff meeting	8:15-8:45 Kdg- Eme 8:45-9:15 Kdg -Dur 9:15-10:15 3 U present posters 10:15-10:45 3T 10:45-11:15 3H Make posters 12:00 Early release day	8:15-8:45 4V Note taking states 8:45-9:15 4MH 9:15-10:45 4CH 10:45-11:15 5C 11:15-11:45 5P 11:30-12:00 Lunch 12:05-12:20 12:30-1:00 5H 1:00-1:30 1W 1:30-2:00 1E 2:00-2:30 1B 2:30-3:00	

Figure 6.2. Sample Fixed Schedule.

Key: KDG-Eme = Kindergarten class, Mrs. Emerson, teacher; KDG-Dur = Kindergarten class, Mrs. Duranski, teacher. Number and letters refer to grade and teacher; for example, 2L is second grade, Mrs. Leu; 1W is first grade, Mrs. White

Week of	Monday	Tuesday	Wednesday	Thursday	Friday
April 5		8:15-8:45 Kdg- Eme 8:45-9:15 Kdg -Dur 9:15-10:15 3 U work on Posters 10:15-10:45 3 T making poster 10:45-11:15 11:30-12:00 Lunch 12:00-12:30 Plan 12:30-1:00 2L Howe 1:00-1:30 2G Parish 1:30-2:00 2K Kline 2:00-2:30 Kdg-Eme 2:30-2:55 Kdg-Dur	3:05 After school supervision	8:15-8:45 4V 8:45-9:15 4MH 9:15-10:45 4CH 10:45-11:15 5C 11:15-11:45 5P 11:30-12:00 Lunch 12:05-12:20\ 12:30-1:00 5H 1:00-1:30 1W 1:30-2:00 1E 2:00-2:30 1B sea animals 2:30-3:00	No School
April 12	No School	8:15-8:45 Kdg- Eme 8:45-9:15 Kdg -Dur 9:15-10:15 3 U Present posters 10:15-10:45 3T work on posters 10:45-11:15 3H Note 11:30-12:00 Lunch 12:00-12:30 Plan 12:30-1:00 2L 1:00-1:30 2G 1:30-2:00 2K 2:00-2:30 Kdg-Eme 2:30-2:55 Kdg-Dur 3:05 Staff meeting		8:15-8:45 4V 8:45-9:15 4MH 9:15-10:45 4CH 10:45-11:15 5C 11:15-11:45 5P 11:30-12:00 Lunch 12:05-12:20 recess 12:30-1:00 5H 1:00-1:30 1W Crews 1:30-2:00 1E Bunting 2:00-2:30 1B Henkes 2:30-3:00	

April 19	8:15-8:45 4V 8:45-9:15 4MH 9:15-10:45 4CH 10:45-11:15 5C 11:15-11:45 5P 11:30-12:00 Lunch 12:05-12:20 12:30-1:00 5H 1:00-1:30 1W 1:30-2:00 1E 2:00-2:30 1B Henkes 2:30-3:00 3:30 LMS W Park		8:15-8:45 4V 8:45-9:15 4MH 9:15-10:45 4CH 10:45-11:15 5C 11:15-11:45 5P 11:30-12:00 Lunch 12:05-12:20 s 12:30-1:00 5H 1:00-1:30 1W 1:30-2:00 1E 2:00-2:30 1B 2:30-3:00	3:05 After school sup 3:45 After school program—Lab
April 26	8:15-8:45 Kdg- Eme 8:45-9:15 Kdg -Dur 9:15-10:15 3 U Present posters 10:15-10:45 3T 10:45-11:15 3H Make posters 11:30-12:00 Lunch 12:00-12:30 Recess 12:30-1:00 2L 1:00-1:30 2G 1:30-2:00 2K 2:00-2:30 Kdg-Eme 2:30-2:55 Kdg-Dur 3:05 staff meeting	12:00 Early release day	8:15-8:45 4V Note taking states 8:45-9:15 4MH 9:15-10:45 4CH 10:45-11:15 5C 11:15-11:45 5P 11:30-12:00 Lunch 12:05-12:20 12:30-1:00 5H 1:00-1:30 1W 1:30-2:00 1E 2:00-2:30 1B 2:30-3:00	

Figure 6.3. Sample Modified Schedule.

Key: KDG-Eme = Kindergarten class, Mrs. Emerson, teacher; KDG-Dur = Kindergarten class, Mrs. Duranski, teacher. Number and letters refer to grade and teacher; for example, 3T is third grade, Mrs. Thomas, 5P is fifth grade, Mrs. Porter.

Making sure that all students use the library media center was a real concern for teachers when flexible scheduling was implemented in one school. To help alleviate their fears, the library media staff agreed to print out once a month the number of items students had checked out (not what they had checked out, but the number of items). Some classroom teachers also put up a book pocket for each student, and when the student had been to the media center and checked out a book, a strip of paper was placed in the pocket. After several years' experience with flexible scheduling the teachers no longer kept a record in their rooms nor did the library staff send reports to the teachers. The practice was discontinued because teachers found that students were continuing to check out books (Jane Dodson, personal experience, 1992). However, the intermediate step of providing proof that students were checking out books was needed to make teachers comfortable with the change.

Meeting the Challenges

The idea of flexible scheduling has to be sold. Library media specialists must be proactive. The support of the principal is essential. Principals indicate that the way they have learned about flexible scheduling is through the library media specialist sharing the experiences with them and providing journal articles supporting its benefits. They describe themselves as cheerleaders, advocates, supporters, communicators, enforcers, promoters, and enablers of flexible scheduling (McGregor, 2003). The selling point for principals is the benefit to students (McGregor, 1999). In planning for flexible scheduling, conducting a needs assessment to find out what services the staff values can help. Then show how flexible scheduling would allow or improve those services. Be sure to include teachers and the principal in decisions.

Providing planning time is a big issue. Using the library media specialist primarily as a teacher ignores the other important contributions the specialist can make to the educational team of the school. A change can be made only when the principal is convinced flexible scheduling will benefit students. After making the decision to have flexible scheduling, one principal extended the lunch period by five minutes each day and held meetings with students at each grade level every other Friday afternoon during which he discussed schoolwide issues or arranged for a presentation by another person (Shannon, 1996). Other schools have added or increased time for computer programs, music, or physical education to provide planning time. One school changed electives by adding rotation option periods. Teachers took turns giving option periods so that they had planning time, but not every day (McGregor, 1999). Another option is to have planning time specified on a weekly rather than a daily basis.

Time to collaborate is a challenge. Teachers and library media specialists are busy. Keep in mind that not every unit requires a detailed meeting between the teacher and the library media specialist. This is especially true if you have collaborated on the unit before. Knowing the teachers also helps. Some teachers want and are more comfortable with a detailed planning meeting for each unit. Other teachers, especially after they get to know you, are willing to let you "just do it" with a minimal amount of collaboration. Then there are teachers who know exactly what they want done and will tell you what they want you to do. For those teachers who don't need a formal meeting, talking at lunch, while walking down the hall, or stopping briefly in the room works fine and takes a minimal amount of time.

Keeping track of which skills have been taught is essential. As Ohlrich (1992) stated, "When the skills are taught is flexible; whether the skills are taught is not flexible." Having a way to track which information literacy skills have been taught, when, and to whom is essential. A binder or database can be used to keep track of which skills have been taught to which classes or grades. (An example is given on p. 62.)

Implementation

Start small. Don't become discouraged. One school tried flexible scheduling for two weeks and found it didn't work. Two weeks is not long enough for teachers to understand the concept, let alone change years of teaching habits. Change takes time—three to five years. McGregor (1999) found in her study that library media specialists recommended looking for the small successes, being persistent, and building over a period of years, not just months.

In order to implement flexible scheduling, the school climate must be one of cooperation and collaboration and must support risk-taking (Shannon, 1996). From her study McGregor (1999) has made the following recommendations to promote successful implementation:

- Visit successful sites together to study how to implement flexible scheduling effectively. Include principals, teachers, and library media specialists.

- Form district committees of teachers to study the concept and bring the findings back to the school.

- Wait for the right time and then seize it. However, waiting might mean years rather than weeks or months.

- Teach teachers to take advantage of the situation.

- Make something happen in the beginning. Actively seek out people with whom to plan, even if only one teacher. Others will follow when they see the advantages of collaborative planning.

- Keep a visible, public schedule so everyone can see what's happening in the media center.

- Loan out rotating and constantly changing classroom libraries to provide regular access to a collection of reading materials to help make sure students have access to them.

- Be able to accept disorganization, uncertainty, and change.

- Be aware that you can't please all the people all the time, and some people may never be advocates of flexible scheduling.

- Be intuitive—figure out where teachers are, meet them wherever they are, and bring them along a continuum of effective use.

- Plan as a district to continually educate new superintendents and administrators.

- Conduct inservices for each other in other schools.

Obviously one will not follow all of these suggestions. What is done depends on the attitude of the teachers and their stages of acceptance of flexible scheduling. Knowing the teachers is an important aspect of implementing flexible scheduling.

Modified Flexible Schedules

A modified flexible schedule is usually adopted because the library media specialist recognizes the benefits of a flexible schedule but is faced by imposed limitations. These limitations could be from having to provide some teacher planning time, being in the building part-time, or teaching another subject. In a modified flexible schedule the library media specialist attempts to provide some time to meet the needs of students and teachers in a limited way. Library media specialists have used the concept of a modified flexible schedule in different ways. For example, on certain days, such as Monday, Wednesday, and Friday, classes are scheduled on a fixed basis. On Tuesday and Thursday the specialist can schedule classes that need additional time. In some cases a certain day of the week or week of the month is designated for flexible scheduling. In other instances a specific class may be designated as the one to have flexible scheduling. In some schools the fifth and sixth grades have flexible schedules, and kindergarten through fourth grades have fixed schedules. The disadvantage to the modified flexible schedule is that it does not automatically provide for individualization, and periodic reinforcement may or may not occur (Karpisek, 1989).

Conclusion

Flexible scheduling is not an end in itself; it is a means to an end. In the case of information literacy, that end is to have students who are literate in finding, using, evaluating, and communicating information. Library media specialists working on fixed schedules should have as a goal moving toward a more flexible scheduling of classes. With flexible scheduling the library media specialist can organize his or her time to teach skills at the point of need; work with students in small groups or independently; confer with teachers; and select, order, and catalog materials for students to use. Flexible scheduling is not an easier way to teach. In fact, as teachers see the benefits of flexible scheduling, the library media specialist will probably find more demands on his or her time. Although it may not be easier, flexible scheduling is a better way to teach because it meets the needs of students and teachers.

CHAPTER 7

It's All About Process

There is more involved in teaching information literacy skills than having a set of standards or objectives. Kuhlthau (1991) found that there is a natural sequence of information use activities that matches children's developmental stages and their need for information arising from their classroom and their personal lives. In pre-kindergarten through fifth grade, learning involves children in asking questions, seeking answers, and sharing their discoveries. Children in fifth through eighth grades are transitioning toward more abstraction in learning (Donham, 2001). Therefore, a sequence of information skills can and needs to be planned. Kuhlthau (1991) further stated that the process of learning from information is at the core of an information literacy program. Information literacy skills taught within a framework of an information process ensure consistent development of needed skills and strategies so that students can retrieve, access, process, and share information (Doiron & Davies, 1998). In other words, students need to learn a process for doing research.

Learning a research process is learning how to solve a problem. Students cannot be taught all the facts they will ever need to know, but they can be taught a process for solving information problems. Knowing how to use a research process is not intuitive; it has to be taught. Pitts (1995) found that a lack of mental models for information seeking was detrimental to the entire research process and to learning from the research task. Students in Ohio schools indicated some fundamentals necessary for them to construct their own understanding of a topic:

- Understanding how to do research effectively

- Understanding how to identify key ideas

- Analyzing, synthesizing and evaluating information

- Structuring and organizing ideas

- Developing personal conclusions. (Todd and Kuhlthau, 2004, p. 20)

83

These fundamentals that students identified are included in most research processes. Once having learned a research process, students are more likely to be independent learners.

There are several research processes or models, but they generally have some steps in common: the research problem, where to find the information, how to extract the information, how to let others know what has been learned, and if the problem has been solved. In addition to learning the steps in a process, there are other positive outcomes. Kuhlthau (1989) found that students came to understand that thinking, reflecting, and mulling were an important part of learning from information. Students also learned that uncertainty is okay at the beginning of all learning. Using a process considers information seeking from the user's point of view.

Research Process

In information literacy, what is being taught is really a research process. Although there are several different processes, they have some basic steps in common.

The Research Problem

The first step is the research problem. This is where students define the keywords or search terms to be used. Defining the problem is a difficult step for students, as they are often accustomed to the teacher telling them what to find. Students need some guidance about what types of questions to ask. According to Moore and St. George (1991), 52 percent of the questions students originally generated were not answered in their final projects. In fact, they substituted questions that fit the information they found. Sometimes, however, the difficulty arises because of the research problem. For many years teachers have asked student to research birds, or something they find interesting about the Civil War. The topics are so broad the students are clueless where to begin. Setting up the right type of research problem is important.

Without the right questions, students won't know where they are going. They won't know which search strategies to use. Questions are needed to cope with the large quantity of information available to students. Students need to understand what they are to do by asking who, what, when, where, why, and how questions.

What is an avalanche?

When is an avalanche likely to occur?

Where is the safest place to be during an avalanche?

Why is an avalanche dangerous?

How can you survive an avalanche?

Brainstorming is often an effective technique to establish questions for an assignment. Then, by using a process to group the questions, some key questions will emerge. Preceding the brainstorming of questions by reviewing what is already known is also a good technique. The review may call to mind some questions. Just as important as what is being learned is relating what is known. From what is known other questions may develop.

Moore and St. George (1991) stated that it is evident that abilities to both reduce and increase the scope of a topic are necessary for the selection of the most appropriate search term. From the generated questions students then can identify keywords to be used in finding and extracting information. Identification of keywords is another skill that needs to be taught. A related learning activity is guiding students in understanding the need for and in thinking of synonyms for the keywords they select.

Finding Information

After determining what questions need to be answered, the student must decide where the best place to look for information is. When asked where to find information, many students will often say, "The Internet." Finding the information needed to answer an information problem is about finding the right source for the questions to be answered. Although students might prefer searching the Internet, they must learn that other sources of information are sometimes more appropriate. The student should ask, "Where is the best place to find this information?" A student needs to know whether a question can be best answered by using an encyclopedia, an almanac, an atlas, or the Internet; by asking an expert; by reading a book; or by looking in the telephone book.

Extracting Information

Once students have decided which resources to use, they must extract the information. Different skills are needed depending on the type of resource they use. The skills for reading and listening are different, as are those for viewing. Students have to be taught some skills for extracting the needed information, such as listening for keywords, using indexes and tables of contents, or searching databases.

Students also have to be taught several ways of taking notes so that they have some options depending on their learning style and the format being used. Visual or graphic organizers work well for many students. A web can help show interconnectivity between two concepts. For some students highlighting passages is most effective. If a student will be interviewing an expert, guidance is needed in developing appropriate questions.

Product/Project

Having gathered the information, students must synthesize and organize it in some manner to convey what they have learned. Frequently teachers determine the product for beginning researchers. However, it is appropriate to familiarize students with different products. Because of interaction with all teachers in the building, the library media specialist can suggest appropriate projects or products to teachers. Although it may be appropriate for very young students to produce products that are basically factual, as they get older students should have projects that require use of critical thinking skills. Having projects that require making inferences and coming to conclusions is practice in using real-life skills.

The product can be almost anything. However, students should complete a variety of products throughout the year. Again, as a person involved in many class learning activities, the library media specialist can suggest products or projects based on what has been done. The most common product is a research paper, but more and more teachers are looking for real-life experience for students to present their findings. Students may be talking to a city council, a parent group, or the principal. At this point the library media specialist and teacher may have to teach how to present information in different formats, for example, PowerPoint presentations, oral presentations, posters, or public service announcements. Using a variety of products recognizes that students have and use multiple intelligences (linguistic, logical-mathematical, spatial, kinesthetic, musical, interpersonal, intrapersonal, and naturalist).

Evaluation

The focus of the evaluation is the research process. Students should think about how the process worked. Was there something they could have done differently that would have made the work easier or improved the product? Should they have looked for more information? Did they run out of time? What would they do differently the next time?

There are a number of ways to evaluate, and not all evaluation has to be formal. Sometimes having students do a self-evaluation by stating what worked best and what would be done differently next time is all that is needed. At other times a rubric may be needed. More about evaluation is covered in Chapter 9.

Research Models

A number of research processes or models have been developed. The key is to find the process that is the best fit with the library media specialist, the teachers, and the students. This chapter attempts to give a brief explanation of some of those most commonly used. All promote critical thinking skills. The description is meant as an introduction to the models, with the idea that the reader will investigate them further.

Big6™

The Big6 is a six-step process developed by Michael B. Eisenberg and Robert E. Berkowitz. Their premise is that most problems have an information component, and that information problems can be solved in a systematic way. The steps seem sequential, but the authors explain that branching is possible and desirable. Each step is broken down into two subskills, which Eisenberg and Berkowitz call the "Little 12." These subskills help explain what is to be done at each step. The steps and the subskills follow:

1. Task definition—defining the task and identifying the information needed to complete the task.

2. Information seeking strategies—identifying the possible resources and selecting the best ones.

3. Location and access—locating sources and finding information within the resources.

4. Use of Information—reading, hearing, viewing in order to extract relevant information.

5. Synthesis—organizing the information and presenting the final project or product in an appropriate format.

6. Evaluation—judging both the process and the product (Eisenberg & Berkowitz, 1999).

This model has great application not only for solving information problems, but also for doing assignments and using in real-life applications.

FLIP IT!™

Developed by Alice Yucht, FLIP was originally a research process but has evolved to being used in other ways. When beginning a research process, FLIP might stand for Focus, Links, Input, and Payoff. For determining research strategies the acronym would mean Focus, Links, Input, and Proprieties. When getting ready to do the research, the letters would stand for Focus topic, Looked in, and Important Points. The teacher might give the students project guidelines that included Focus, Layout, Input, and Pay attention to. There is even a FLIP for assessment—Focus, Logistics, Information content, and Presentation.

The IT stands for If/Then, which is an important part of the process as it helps students make connections between the steps. For example, IF the Focus is on a Native American tribe, THEN what Links or resources are needed to answer the questions? IT also stands for Intelligent Thinking throughout the process. The student reflects on whether or not the final product answered the questions. Were the best resources used? Were the questions appropriate? Was time used wisely?

The steps, with an explanation for the different FLIP IT uses, follow.

Beginning a research project with FLIP IT!

1. Focus—think about the topic to be researched and ask what information they needed to complete the project; narrow the topic

2. Links—what resources are needed to answer the questions? What is the logical way to proceed

3. Input—what kinds of information needs to be found? What is the best way to organize and use the information gathered? How is the information to be recorded? Is more information needed?

4. Payoff—how can the student show what has been learned or the problem has been solved?

IT—how has the student demonstrated Intelligent Thinking throughout the process?

Planning research strategies with FLIP IT!

1. Focus—keywords and search terms to be used

2. Links—locations and call numbers of resources

3. Input—kinds of information needed; note taking, copying biblio-graphic information

4. Proprieties—use a variety of resources, share materials, put mate-rials away

IT—how has the student demonstrated Intelligent Thinking throughout the process?

Researching with FLIP IT!
This is the note-taking stage of research.

1. Focus topics—list all the topics for which information is needed with a letter (A, B, C, etc.)

2. Looked in—list resources used, each with a symbol (#, $, *).

3. Important Points—lower left hand side of paper is numbered 1–5 and right hand side is numbered 6–10. Notes are written here. With each note is written the letter of the topic and the symbol of the re-source (Yucht, 1999).

IT—how has the student demonstrated Intelligent Thinking throughout the process?

Figure 7.1 (p. 90) is an example of the note-taking stage for a student do-ing research on Benjamin Franklin. Students are asked to fold a piece of paper into fourths. The top left fourth contains topics to research, the top right fourth is for sources and the bottom half is for the notes.

Information Search Process

Carol Kuhlthau, an early researcher into the information search process, looked at the development of student thoughts about a topic and the feelings that accompany those thoughts. Kuhlthau developed the Information Search Process from five studies she conducted. Each of the seven stages in the pro-cess includes tasks, thoughts, feelings, actions, and strategies that students commonly experience. The tasks are listed, but only some of the feelings, ac-tions, and strategies are included as examples (Kuhlthau, 1994b).

Focus Topics	Sources:
A. Political views	& Brands, H. W. *The First American.* New York: Anchor Books, 2000.
B. Personality	# Ellis, Joseph J. *Founding Brothers.* New York: Vintage Books, 2000.
C. Contributions to government	% "The Autobiography of Benjamin Franklin". *Early America Review.* [On-line] Available, http://www.earlyamerica.com/lives/franklin Assessed 2003.

Important	Points
1. One of 8 most prominent political leaders C#	6. Used situations to make money B%
2. Negotiated alliance with France C#	7. Printed newspaper, ran stationery B%
3. Led antislavery movement 1787 A#	8.
4. Intelligent; not tolerate less intelligence B&	9.
5. Enjoyed English society & intellectuals B&	10.

Figure 7.1. FLIP IT. (Based on a process developed by Alice Yucht.)

1.   Initiating a research assignment: The problem is introduced.

   Students are frequently confused and uncertain as to what they are to do. Strategies include brainstorming, discussing, and contemplating possible topics.

2.   Selecting a topic: Discussing or considering possible topics for investigation.

   Actions would include talking with others, making a preliminary search of the library media collection, and using the encyclopedia to determine what is available. After selecting a topic students have a big feeling of elation.

3.   Exploring information: Reading to become informed about the broad topic

   At this step students would identify several possible focuses for research. They would look for interesting facts and ideas and make bibliographic citations. This is often the most difficult part of the process.

4. Formulating a focus: Forming a focus for the investigation.

    Students look at their choices and decide which looks the most promising. Having chosen a focus, students can plan a strategy for finding information. Students move from feelings of uncertainty to understanding.

5. Collecting information: Seeking information to define, extend, and support the focus.

    Students begin taking detailed notes. From the notes a narrative begins to take shape.

6. Preparing to present: Concluding the search for information and planning the product.

    Students organize their notes and synthesize the information into a draft. After making a final copy, which includes a bibliography, the product is presented. At this point students experience a sense of relief.

7. Assessing the process: Identifying the problems and successes of the process

    In evaluating the process students would seek evidence of the focus in the product, assess the use of time, and evaluate the resources used. Students have a sense of accomplishment at this point.

One of the strong features of this model is the reflective aspect. As they progress through the process, students are to asked certain questions that help them reflect on their progress and success to date by keeping a journal of the research process. Kuhlthau (1994b) feels that writing helps students formulate their ideas, clarify their thinking, and become aware of the progress they are making. The journal will also help in the assessment stage.

Pathways to Knowledge®

Pathways to Knowledge®, developed by Marjorie Pappas and Ann E. Tepe, is an information process that provides both stages and strategies for solving information problems. All but the first stage have function statements. For each function statement there are general strategies that help implement the function statement. The steps with their function statements follow:

1. Appreciation

2. Pre-search
    Establishing my focus

3. Search
    Planning and implementing my search strategy

4. Interpretation
    Assessing usefulness of my information
    Reflecting to develop my personal meaning

5. Communication
    Constructing and presenting my new knowledge

6. Evaluation
    Thinking about my product and process (Pappas, 2000).

Although appreciation is the first step in this model, it is not mandatory. Appreciation often develops as a student conducts the research, draws conclusions, and presents the product. However, appreciation may never become apparent or develop for the student. At the pre-search stage teachers and library media specialists give students time to make connections between the topic, what they need to know, and what they already know. The search stage is where students determine what resources they will use, evaluate their usefulness, and take notes. During the interpretation stage students reflect on and internalize the information. Communication includes organizing the information and presenting in to others. At the evaluation stage an evaluation of the product and the research process is done. However, in the Pathways model peer and self- evaluation are encouraged throughout the process.

Research Process

This ten-step process, developed by Barbara K. Stripling and Judy M. Pitts, suggests a sequence. Research is described as a thinking activity: students are asked at certain steps to reflect on what they have done. The ten steps are explained below.

"1. Choose a broad topic"

This step is usually assigned by the teacher until students become proficient at researching.

"2. Get an overview of the topic"

In the beginning the teacher might give the overview. Students would then progress to overviews being discussed in class, then to doing individual readings.

"3. Narrow the topic"

Beginning researchers often narrow their topics by drawing or selecting from a teacher list. As students progress in their research abilities they will be able to narrow topics based on their personal interests and information available.

"*Reflection Point:* Is my topic a good one?"

"4. Develop thesis/purpose statement"

Teachers usually assign beginning researchers a thesis statement, but students progress to writing statements after class discussion, then to independently writing a purpose statement.

"*Reflection Point:* Does my thesis or statement of purpose represent an effective, overall concept for my research?"

"5. Formulate questions to guide research"

After initial instruction, students formulate questions as a class, then individually, and progress to being able to write questions independently with guidance.

"*Reflection Point:* Do the questions provide a foundation for my research?"

"6. Plan for research and production"

As beginning researchers students are told what the product will be and what exactly is to be included. After much experience students should be able to determine what type of product will best present the information and know what skills are needed to produce the product and how long it will take.

"*Reflection Point:* Is the research/production plan workable?"

"7. Find, analyze, evaluate sources"

What and how many resources to use are usually predetermined by the teacher for beginning researchers. More experienced students will be able to select appropriate resources based on some criteria they have learned.

"*Reflection Point:* Are my sources usable and adequate?"

"8.   Evaluate evidence, take notes/compile bibliography"

With instruction students will learn a variety of ways to take notes. As they become experienced in note taking, students use a format they choose. With experience students will also be able to evaluate whether or not a resource is suitable for their needs.

"Reflection Point: Is my research complete?"

"9.   Establish conclusions/organize into an outline"

As they begin learning the research process, students will need help organizing the information. Often this step is done as a class, with students inserting their own information. Students then progress to being able to organize on their own, then with guidance, then to being fairly independent.

"Reflection Point: Are my conclusions based on researched evidence? Does my outline logically organize conclusions and evidence?"

"10.   Create and present final product"

The final product is prepared and presented according to steps outlined by the teacher or library media specialist as the student begins learning the research process. As they become more experienced, students will have more say in what the final product is. Competent researchers will express their own creativity in their products.

"Reflection Point: Is my paper/project satisfactory?" (Stripling & Pitts, 1988, p. 20)

Research Cycle

Jamie McKenzie, who created this model, feels that asking the right question is essential. If the researcher starts with good questions, the rest will follow more easily. The seven activities of the cycle follow:

1.   Questioning—clarifying the essential question being explored; developing questions around the central theme

2.   Planning—finding pertinent and reliable information; where information can be found, what the best source for the information is, if the source is available, if it will answer the questions

3.   Gathering—pulling together and sorting according to topic the resources to be used; taking notes

4.   Sorting and sifting—organizing data to contribute insight into the original information problem

5. Synthesizing—arranging and rearranging the information to arrive at a conclusion

6. Evaluating—whether the information problem has been answered; if more research is needed

7. Reporting—sharing what was found with others (McKenzie, 2000).

Implementing a Research Process

A research process is not a curriculum. The process is the way by which the information literacy skills are taught in collaboration with other teachers. No matter what the topic, students will learn more if the lesson follows an information problem-solving model and the principles of learning. The first step in implementing a research process is to adopt one that will be used throughout the school, if not the district. With all teachers using the same process, students get repeated practice in applying it. With practice the process becomes automatic. In addition, since everyone uses the same model, teachers can share the responsibility of teaching the process, thus taking less time from teaching other curricula. Students tend to move within a district and certainly progress within a district; therefore, having the same process used K–12 provides some consistency for students and prevents them having to spend time learning a new model.

As with any change, adopting a research model does not "just happen." First of all, the library media specialist needs the support and cooperation of the principal. Curriculum directors are also important stakeholders in adoption. Administrators need to see benefits from using a research model. Tying the research process to district and building goals is imperative. Explain how a research process will help the district or school meet its goals. Another area to target is state standards. Some states have information literacy standards, others include information literacy in standards for other subject areas, and still others have nothing in terms of information literacy standards. Regardless, a review of the standards in all subject areas is important to be prepared to demonstrate how a research process can help students meet those standards.

Once administrators see the benefit to using a research process, they will lead the way to including teachers in the decision-making process. Teachers will have to be convinced of the value of a research process in much the same way administrators have been. Once they too see the importance, move to a discussion of which model to choose. The library media specialist and some classroom teachers might investigate the different models and discuss the strengths and weaknesses in using them with the students. In some cases the models might even be tried with students before one is adopted.

Once the decision has been made about which research process to use, some inservice will have to be conducted. Carefully select who will present the model to the teachers, because that person must have credibility with all teachers. The presenter could be the library media specialist, the principal, a respected fellow teacher, or someone from outside the school or district. If the process is being used in another school within the district, invite the library media specialist and a teacher to present the process to the faculty. Regardless of who conducts the inservice, the library media specialist must thoroughly understand the process and how to teach it, because he or she will have to be readily available to help and encourage teachers in its use.

The teachers need to know the steps in the process, but they also need to understand how the process integrates with what is already being taught. Teaching research skills should not be an added class, but rather an enhancement that helps students succeed in their learning. Different parts of the research process are emphasized in different assignments. While presenting an inservice to a middle school staff on integrating the research process, the teachers at one school were concerned about when they were going to teach the process. The question asked was, "How can we teach this? We already have more to cover than we can get done." The answer was twofold. First, integrate the process into a current assignment. Second, the entire process is not taught in all classes. Emphasize particular steps in particular assignments. The library media specialist is central in helping teachers know what has been done in other classes (Joie Taylor, personal experience, 1998).

Inservice might also be important for the para-educators in the school. Because they work with students, para-educators must understand the research process as well as how to use the various computer programs and search engines available to students. In one school, after a meeting of all the schools' para-educators, the library assistant relayed to the library media specialist the desire of the para-educators to have some training in the computer programs that were being used in student projects (Kathi Nelson, personal communication, 2004).

Tying the Research Process to Information Literacy Skills

The research process gives students a set of skills to solve information problems, but like information literacy skills, they are not taught in isolation. The process is the framework around which the information literacy skills are taught. Following are examples of information literacy skills based on the Big6 skills, written by two school districts. They look different because the development was necessarily different. In developing information literacy skills, it is important that the district model for curriculum be followed.

The first example is more like the basic scope and sequence that some districts use. The curriculum committee had as members an administrator, four classroom teachers representing the elementary, middle, and high schools, and one library media specialist from each level. Five performance goals were determined, and suggested activities were listed for each. Following that a determination was made about when each activity would be I—introduced, P—practiced, M—mastered, and R—reinforced. The terms introduce, practice, master, and reinforce had been used in other district curricula, but the team created a fourth level, A—add. The add level was to indicate that even though a skill had been mastered there were additional or new aspects of the skill that needed to be learned. An example is searching databases. Even though students knew how to use keywords for searching, they still might need to learn how to use a specific database.

The five performance goals were:

1. Define the information need (problem) and choose the best resources.

2. Locate specific resources and information within them.

3. Use (read, hear, view) the resources and extract the needed information.

4. Organize the information from all resources and create a product.

5. Share the product based on a research project (Columbus, 1998).

Figure 7.2 (p. 98) is an example of how the scope and sequence is written. The scope and sequence is used mostly by the library media specialists to give them an overall picture at a glance. Each teacher is given a copy of the information literacy skills appropriate for his or her grade level, but the format is different because it follows the one used for all curricula in the district. See Figure 7.3 (p. 99) for an example.

Information Literacy Scope & Sequence

Performance goal 2: The learner will locate specific resources and information within them.

Suggested Activity	K	1	2	3	4	5	6	7	8	9	10	11	12
Locate specific resources:													
A. Locate resources within library media Center (intellectually/physically):													
1. Know the location and purpose of the library media center	I	P	P	P	P	M	R	R	R	R	R	R	R
2. Identify areas of the library media center, e.g., fiction, circulation desk, everybody	I	P	P	P	P	M	R	R	R	R	R	R	R
3. Comprehend that the call number tells where the item is located and relates the call number to the location of materials on the shelf in a specific order			I	P	P	M	R	R	R	R	R	R	R
a. Dewey Decimal Number and author (Cutter number in high school)				I	P	M	R	R	R	A	A	A	A
b. Biography — Can use on-line catalog to tell if a book is a biography				I	P	M	A	A	A	A	A	A	A
c. Reference				I	P	M	A	A	A	A	A	A	A
d. A-V resources				I	P	M	A	A	A	A	A	A	A
4. Identify left to right, top to bottom shelf arrangement			I	P	P	M	R	R	R	R	R	R	R
5. Scan immediate area for resources on similar subjects or misshelved items					I	M	R	R	R	R	R	R	R
6. Comprehend that the online catalog is an index to print and nonprint materials in the library media center			I	P	P	M	R	R	R	R	R	R	R
7. Apply the ability to use computer to the online catalog using key words, author, title, or subject			I	P	P	M	A	A	A	A	A	A	A
8. Apply the ability to search by key words in sources of information				I	P	M	A	A	A	A	A	A	A
9. Use Boolean search strategies				I	P	M	A	A	A	A	A	A	A

I = Introduce   P = Practice   M = Master   A = Additional instruction beyond basic skill mastery

Figure 7.2. Information Literacy Scope and Sequence. (Used with the permission of the Columbus (NE) Public Schools library media specialists.)

Goal Two—The Learner will locate specific resources and information within them.

Reinforce	**Know the location and purpose of the library media center.**
Reinforce	Identify areas of the library media center and other places where they might obtain information.
Reinforce	Comprehend that the call number on materials tells where the item is located and relates the call number to the location of materials on shelf in a specific order.
Add	Locate Dewey Decimal Number, Cutter Number
Add	Know how to use online catalog to tell if a book is a biography.
Add	Know the location of the reference materials.
Add	Know the location and purpose of the A-V resources.
Reinforce	Identifies left to right, top to bottom shelf arrangement.
Reinforce	Scans immediate area for resources on similar subjects or for mis-shelved items.
Reinforce	Comprehend that the computer catalog is an index to print and nonprint materials in the library media center.
Add	Apply the ability to use computer to search the automated catalog using key words, author, title or subject.
Add	Apply the ability to search by key words in sources of information.
Add	Use Boolean search strategies.
Reinforce	Locate resources outside library media center (intellectually/physically)
Reinforce	Apply knowledge of checking out and returning resources.
Reinforce	Demonstrate procedures for reserving resources.
Reinforce	Demonstrate procedures for interlibrary loaning resources.
Add	Know that most resources have an internal organizational system such as Indexes, Guide Words, Table of Contents, Main Menu, HyperLinks, Search engines, cross references, search screen, graphic clues.
Reinforce	Apply use of alphabetizing skills.
Reinforce	Locate major headings/groupings.
Reinforce	Identify keywords and phrases within resources.
Reinforce	Know the cover, spine, title page, and verso.
Reinforce	Know the page/verso information—author, title, illustrator, copyright, publisher, place of publication, and editor.

Goal Three—TLW use (read, hear, view) the resources and extract the needed information.

Master	**Operate the technology needed to access information.**
Master	**Skim and scan resources for key ideas.**
Master	**Use more than one source to find information on a topic to help determine accuracy.**
Master	**Recognize the difference between fact and opinion.**
Master	**Determines comprehensiveness of the information.**
Master	**Record pertinent information by note taking, charting, graphical aids, highlighting.**
Master	**Recognize that information can be moved from one document to another.**

**Figure 7.3. Information Literacy Skills—Grade 11
(Columbus Public Schools, 1998).**

The library media specialists have made a connection between the scope and sequence and the research process. Figure 5.2 (see pp. 62–64) shows how the skills and the process are related. The first column is the research process; the second column is the information literacy activity. In the first column 1TD means Step 1—Task Definition in the Big6 process. Likewise, 2ISS is Step 2—Information Seeking Strategies; 4UofI is Step 4—Use of Information; 5Syn is Step 5—Synthesis; and 6Eval is Step 6—Evaluation. The absence of any objectives associated with step 3, location and access, does not mean this step is totally ignored. As appropriate the library media specialist will instruct and reinforce this skill.

In the second example, the Lincoln Public Schools, has also made a connection between information literacy skills and the Big6, but the format is different. The skills have been divided into four areas:

- Orientation to information resources

- Selection and utilization of resources

- Organization and presentation of information

- Information and literature appreciation

Specific skills have been listed in each of the four areas for grades Pre-K–2, 3–5, 6–8, and 9–12. Following are examples from the skills for Orientation to Information Resources. The learner

- Knows that resources can be obtained for pleasure and for information from various locations (school library media centers and public libraries, on-line, community, etc.)

- Identifies and locates appropriate materials and hardware that meet his/her needs.

- Knows that there are tools available that organize information for location (card on-line catalog, home page, etc.)

- Knows the various types of library media center hardware and software and online resources used in gathering information.

- Uses library catalog independently to locate materials by author, title, or subject.

- Applies knowledge that the periodical section consists of magazines for pleasure reading and other materials that provide current information.

- Knows that the purpose of the Dewey Decimal system is to classify and arrange nonfiction materials by subject. (Lincoln, 2003, p. 15)

Instead of linking a skill with a specific step in the Big6, an Information Literacy Research Path was developed, which has three components: research steps, learner strategies, and instructional strategies. The research steps are the six steps to be followed for informational problem solving, with explanations and action verbs. For example, under Task Definition students would be guided to think about what needs to be done and what information is needed, and to identify needed information. The learner strategies provide questions that the students can ask themselves to help them complete each of the steps. Here students would identify keywords or concepts and other related topics and consider what resources might be available, whether the topic was too broad or too narrow, and what is already known. The instructional strategies are tools or actions to be taught that will help students complete each of the six steps. Here are listed instructional strategies for the library media specialist, including brainstorm, webbing, discuss, create possible questions, model, and list (Lincoln, 2003).

Conclusion

Examining and selecting a research process is important to the instruction of information literacy skills for a number of reasons. According to Donham and others, a research process helps to

- Analyze and break down a process so lessons can be designed to teach it

- Provide a common language for communication among library media specialists, teachers, and students

- Guide students in the research process

- Help library media specialists and teachers monitor what's taught and what students learn (2001, p. 16)

Todd (1995) found that there is value in both a process approach and an integrated approach to information skills instruction, in other words, a research process along with information literacy skills integrated in other curricula.

A research process requires instruction and practice so that it becomes automatic. A resourced-based curriculum provides the best avenue for utilizing a research model. Inquiry-based, project-based, or problem-based learning activities require using a research process. When students have a research model to use, learning is perceived as a process rather than a product. Knowing the process model allows students to continue learning after leaving school.

CHAPTER 8

Setting the Stage for Learning

Information literacy can be considered a basic survival skill for the 21st century. Since information needs arise in the real world from various situations, information literacy skills should be taught within the realm of real-world problems and placed within the context of the overall learning process (authentic learning). Attention should also be given to the way students learn. The study of how humans learn has revealed much about the process of learning. For students to achieve maximum understanding of what is being taught, the library media specialist must consider both how students learn and various processes for structuring learning activities.

How Humans Learn: A Brief Introduction

In *We're Born to Learn*, Rita Smilkstein (2003) states that the human brain is designed to learn and wants to learn. As evidence she points to how almost all humans learn to walk and talk without formal instruction. Smilkstein says there are six natural learning stages that educators would do well to heed when designing curriculum and learning activities:

1. Motivation—Respond to stimulus in the environment

2. Beginning Practice—Practice; train and error; learn from mistakes

3. Advanced Practice—More practice, resulting in increase of skill and confidence

4. Skillfulness—Practice in new ways; share what is known

5. Refinement—Learn new methods; show creativity; skill has become a habit and can teach others

6. Mastery—Continue to get better by meeting greater challenges; transfer skill to other interests

Describing exactly how the brain learns is beyond the scope of this book. However, a brief description is in order. In order to learn the brain must grow dendrites, which look something like the roots of a plant. The various dendrites connect with each other at points called synapses. The growing and connecting of dendrites is learning. In order to learn, humans must link new learning with something already known, but in the process also change what is known. Learning takes time because the growing of dendrites, synapses, and the resulting neural networks takes time.

Not only must new learning be connected to something known, the learning should be a stimulating experience. Stimulating experiences arouse the brain to seek patterns, solve problems, and understand how the world works, and they cause the neural structure to grow and connect. Once learned, practice must be continued, because one rule of the brain is "something not practiced is lost." However, learning that has been used for a long period of time is not lost as fast as learning that is practiced for only a short period of time. As a way to illustrate this rule, someone who has ridden a bike for 15 years and then does not ride for 10 will easily take to riding again. On the other hand, someone who just learned to balance and ride around the block and then stopped riding the bike will need to do a great deal of learning after 10 years.

Learning is specific to the situation in which the learning occurred. This fact helps explain why students can punctuate sentences in language arts classes but not in social studies. The skill has to be practiced in different situations, making connections to what is already known in order for students to learn to transfer the learning from one situation to another. Transfer of learning is not automatic. Students must be taught how to make the transfer by using the new skill in different situations.

There is much more to know about how humans learn, and the reader is referred to Smilkstein's book or others on the topic. The purpose for this discussion is to show that there is a scientific basis for integrating information literacy skills into other curricular areas. If students are to learn and use a research process, they must learn the process in connection with something that is known. Westwater and Wolfe (2000) state that information the brain determines is important is more likely to be attended to, stored, and later retrieved. The brain makes that determination on the basis of a recognizable pattern or feature, or what is already known. People then use what is known in a new way. The process must be used many times in different settings. If the research process is used only in language arts, students will think of it only in terms of language arts. In order for the research or information process to be a life-long skill, students must experience using it in science, math, social studies, art, doing homework, and setting up for homecoming.

Structuring Learning Activities

How does a library media specialist design learning experiences that will stimulate the brain to learn? The strongest neural networks are formed from actual experiences; therefore, students should be involved in authentic problems in their school or community (Westwater & Wolfe 2000). For students authentic learning involves exploring the world around them, asking questions, discovering connections, examining multiple perspectives, discussing ideas, and making informed decisions that have a real impact (Callison & Lamb, 2004, p. 34). Authentic learning experiences have the added advantage of helping students see how reading, writing, and mathematics are used in ordinary life experiences.

There are various terms to describe the different ways authentic learning activities can be structured. Some educators use *problem-based learning* (Schroeder & Zarinnia, 2001), while others use *resource-based learning* (California School Library Association, 1997), *inquiry-based learning* (Donham et al., 2001), or *constructivism* (Perkins, 1999). There is also *project-based learning*. These concepts do have some common features, and all are conducive to teaching information literacy skills and are based on teaching subject content objectives also. In all of them, there is an information problem or need, a variety of resources in various formats must be used, information must be extracted from the resources and then synthesized, a solution must be determined and communicated in an acceptable format, and the solution and process must be evaluated. Figure 8.1 (p. 106) compares problem-based, inquiry-based, project-based, and resource-based learning.

The excitement for students is learning centered in solving a problem or addressing an issue they find meaningful. A meaningful issue activates the brain's mechanisms to learn. What makes learning real? Harada and Kim (2003) suggest the following characteristics of meaningful learning:

- Deals with a problem or issue with which kids can connect

- Allows for students making choices

- Involves hands-on and minds-on tasks

- Requires problem solving in teams or groups

- Results in sharing new knowledge with real audiences

Learning with these characteristics takes advantage of the brain's natural tendency to want to learn.

Problem-Based	Inquiry-Based	Project-Based	Resource-Based
Focus is on process of solving a problem and acquiring knowledge.	Focus is on self-identification of information need.	Focus is on developing a product as the result of investigation.	Focus is on using resources to facilitate learning.
Identify information problem or need.	Identify information problem or need.	Identify information problem or need.	Identify information problem or need.
Determine search strategy.	Determine search strategy.	Determine search strategy.	Determine search strategy.
Extract information from resources.	Extract information from resources.	Extract information from resources.	Extract information from resources.
Collect and organize information.	Collect and organize information.	Collect and organize information.	Collect and organize information.
	Relate information to original questions.	Construct meaning from questions.	Interpret the information.
Create product or performance.	Present solution to information question.	Create a product to demonstrate learning.	Communicate the information.
Assess and evaluate work.	Assess process and solution.	Assess process and product.	Evaluate conclusion in relation to original problem.

Figure 8.1. Comparison of Authentic Learning Activities.

Problem-Based Learning

In problem-based learning students focus on the process of solving a problem and acquiring knowledge. According to Harada and Kim (2003), problem-based learning includes

- identifying the problem or issue,

- discussion of the reasons and implications presented by the problem, and

- discussion of how to solve or improve the situation.

There is a natural correlation between problem-based learning and information literacy. Harada and Kim (2003) identify the teaching and learning steps as follows:

- Identify the big or essential questions addressed by the problem (motivation).

- Find out what students already know (tie to existing knowledge).

- Agree on how to assess the final solution.

- Brainstorm what information is needed and how to find it (practice).

- Collect and organize information (more practice).

- Create a product or performance (practice in new ways).

- Continually assess and evaluate work (learning new ways).

- Consider the next steps. How could the solution be used in another situation (mastery)?

The terms in parentheses show the correlation between problem-based learning and the steps in the brain's learning process.

Schroeder and Zarinnia (2001) demonstrate a parallel between problem-based learning and information literacy skills. In Figure 8.2 (p. 108) the brain's learning stages have been added to show how these fit with information literacy skills.

Resource-Based Learning

Resource-based learning is not to be confused with resource-based teaching. In resource-based teaching the teacher uses a variety of resources to instruct students. Students may not actually use the resources. In resource-based learning the focus is on the students using a variety of resources to facilitate their own learning. This model differs from the other approaches to learning in that the focus is more on the resources than the learning experience. Learning that is resource-based provides information seeking, evaluating, and organizing opportunities (Thompson & Henley, 2000, p. 67).

Students are active learners under the guidance of teachers. Questions are formulated and follow a trail of other questions. The students find the information and turn it into knowledge by making their own meanings from a variety of resources. A general process for resource-based learning is to

1. define the need for information (motivation),

2. determine a search strategy (practice),

3. locate needed resources (practice),

4. assess and understand the information (more practice),

5. interpret the information (practice in new ways),

6. communicate the information (learning new ways), and

7. evaluate the conclusion in relation to the original problem (mastery) (ASCD, 1995).

Problem-based Learning	Information Literacy	Learning Stages
Encounters ill-defined problem	State information need	Motivation
Define sub-problems Develop hypotheses	Define need	Practice
Determine: • What do I know? • What do I need to know?	Explore relationship	Practice
Where can I find the information needed? How can I find information from different perspectives?	Develop search strategy	More practice
Gather information from various sources	Locate and use resource	More practice
Share and analyze data Revisit hypothesis, seek more information if needed, make recommendation	Select, interpret, analyze synthesize, and evaluate information	Practice in new ways
Agree on solution and defend in authentic forum Generalize to wider context	Present/communicate knowledge	Learning new ways
Self-assessment Assess product	Evaluate product and process	Mastery

Figure 8.2. Information Literacy and Stages of Learning.

Again, the terms in the parentheses show the correlation to the brain's natural learning process.

Like other methods of learning, resource-based learning helps students develop information literacy skills. There are also some other benefits to students in using a resource-based type of learning:

- Increased autonomy of learning;

- Mimicry of real life, where the learner constructs knowledge from the resources based on the questions to be answered;

- In-depth focus on a topic, which results in higher quality of learning;

- Promotion of thinking skills through the interaction with information in a variety of formats; and

- Better student attitude toward learning.

Inquiry-Based Learning

When students learn through an inquiry-based approach they focus on questioning, critical thinking, and problem solving just as they do in the other methods. The difference between problem-based and inquiry-based learning is that in inquiry-based learning students help create or identify the problem. Students may even initiate the original question in relation to a class assignment or something happening in school or in the community. In inquiry-based learning the teacher might also create a real or hypothetical real-world problem for students to solve.

Questioning does not stop with the initial or main question. The role of the library media specialist is to guide and encourage the students to continue to ask questions throughout the information search process. Because the questions have been identified by the students, they are more enthusiastic when it comes to finding the answers, answers that are not given facts, but that must be constructed from the information that is found. Another benefit to inquiry-based learning is that a variety of learning modes can be accommodated.

Project-Based Learning

The project-based approach to learning is focused on developing a product or creation as the result of an in-depth investigation of a real-world topic. The project could be student-centered, problem-based, or inquiry-based, but it doesn't necessarily have to be any of those. The student, often working in a small group, constructs meaning from questions that result in carefully designed products. Resolving the questions will help students learn the curriculum content.

The Buck Institute for Education (2002) discusses project-based learning as a way to meet standards. The Institute identifies the following characteristics of effective projects:

- Project work is central rather than peripheral to the curriculum.

- Issues or questions lead students to in-depth exploration of important topics.

- Essential tools and skills are used for learning, self-management, and project management.

- Products solve problems, explain dilemmas, or present information generated through investigation, research, or reasoning.

- Multiple products permit frequent feedback and consistent opportunities for students to learn from experience.

- Performance-based assessments communicate high expectations, present rigorous challenges, and require a range of skills and knowledge.

- There is collaboration, either through small groups, student-led presentations, or whole-class evaluations of project results.

Project-based learning is not appropriate for teaching certain basic skills such as reading and math, but it is appropriate for those situations requiring higher order thinking skills and critical thinking. The Buck Institute for Education (2002) lists the following benefits of project-based learning:

- It overcomes the dichotomy between knowledge and thinking, helping students to both "know" and "do."

- It supports students in learning and practicing skills in problem solving, communication, and self-management.

- It encourages the development of habits of mind associated with life-long learning, civic responsibility, and personal or career success.

- It integrates curriculum areas, thematic instruction, and community issues.

- It assesses performance on content and skills using criteria similar to those in the work world, thus encouraging accountability, goal setting, and improved performance.

- It creates positive communication and collaborative relationships among diverse groups of students.

- It meets the needs of learners with varying skill levels and learning styles.

- It engages and motivates bored or indifferent students.

The Essential Question

One common feature in most of the types of learning discussed above is the importance of asking questions. Questions are important in student achievement (Black et al., 2004). Black and others state that more time has to be spent on framing questions that are worth asking, questions that explore issues critical to the development of student understanding. Such questions help stimulate the brain's natural desire to know, understand, or make sense of a problem. McKenzie (2001) calls these essential questions and defines them as questions that help us make meaning out of the events and circumstances of our lives. The essential questions are at the center of all other types of questions. Brainstorming is a technique that is often used to develop questions related to the essential question.

McKenzie (2000) has identified several of these related questions, which he calls subsidiary questions:

- Hypothetical questions—designed to explore possibilities and test relationships

- Telling questions—help students gather only the information needed

- Planning questions—help students structure their searches

- Organizing questions—help structure findings that allow construction of meaning

- Probing questions—get students beyond the surface of investigation

- Sorting and sifting questions—allow sorting out of the important information and getting rid of the unessential

- Clarification questions—define and create logical meaning

- Strategic questions—focus on ways to make meaning

- Elaborating questions—extend and stretch the import of what is being found

- Unanswerable questions—help students push the limits

- Inventive questions—rearrange information until a new insight or discovery is found

- Provocative questions—push, and challenge and cause students to look at information in new ways

- Irrelevant questions—distract, and cause students to venture away from conventional thinking

- Divergent questions—explore existing knowledge in terms adjacent to common meanings

- Irreverent questions—explore that which is off-limits or taboo

Another way to look at questioning is in terms of Bloom's taxonomy. The Maryland State Department of Education (2004) has developed questions for each level of the taxonomy. Following are some of these.

Knowledge: Who, what, when, where, how?

Comprehension: What is the main idea of

Application: How is _____ an example of _____?
                 How is _____ related to _____?
                 Why is _____ significant?

Analysis: What are the parts or features of _____?
                 How does _____ compare/contrast with _____?
                 What evidence can you present for _____?

Synthesis: What would you predict/infer from _____?
                 What ideas can you add to _____?
                 What solutions would you suggest for _____?

Evaluation: Why do you agree with _____?
                 Which is most important? _____
                 Which criteria would you use to assess _____?

The Importance of Critical Thinking

One of the important outcomes of information literacy skills is developing in students the ability to think critically. What does this mean, and how does the library media specialist accomplish this important task? One definition of critical thinking is the application, analysis, synthesis, and evaluation of information so it can be used to construct personal meaning (Laverty, 1998).

In the information literacy curriculum, the idea is to help students develop thinking strategies as an integral part of what is being learned rather than teaching thinking as a discrete unit. A group of experts determined six core critical thinking skills: analysis, inference, explanation, interpretation, evaluation, and self-regulation (Facione, 1998). These six skills are to be taught along with information literacy. There is a natural fit. As students extract information from resources, they need to analyze what is said, make inferences, and evaluate the usefulness of the information. Having found the needed information, students are required to draw conclusions through inference, explanation, and interpretation.

Incorporating the teaching of thinking skills is not difficult. The learning strategies used to teach any content can also be used to teach thinking skills. Common strategies that can be used include

- keeping journals,

- asking questions and refining the original questions,

- considering what is already known,

- using graphic organizers,

- evaluating resources in terms of information needs,

- working in groups, and

- presenting what is learned.

The teaching of a research process is a natural way of teaching critical thinking skills. There are questions that are naturally asked in connection to research. Starting with the original information problem, the student must analyze the problem to determine exactly what information is needed. Resources have to be evaluated to determine whether they meet the information need, represent a certain viewpoint, or are accurate. Data in charts and tables must be interpreted. Inferences can be drawn from visuals, or in the case of interviews from facial expressions and tone of voice. Always there is the element of self-regulation. Do I have enough information? Is the presentation appropriate for the audience? What is the best way to present the information?

Restructuring the Learning Environment

Whether the *resource-based learning, inquiry-learning, project-based, or problem-based learning* is used, there must be a fundamental change in instruction in order to take advantage of the way humans learn. The focus shifts from the teacher directing all learning to the teacher guiding learning and the students being more involved in directing their own learning. This change of focus has been described as the teacher moving from the sage on the stage to the guide on the side. This change in focus requires some restructuring within the school.

The learning environment must be restructured. Any restructuring must first have the support of the building principal. Information literacy skills must be integrated with other curricula to ensure that those skills are developed and nurtured when students need them. The classroom teacher and the library media specialist must collaborate to see that information literacy skills are taught. In their study of Colorado libraries Lance and others (1993) found that when library media specialists collaborate with classroom teachers, student achievement improves. Further, learning activities should be assigned so students connect with resources in a meaningful way. Resources must be available when students need them, which requires flexible scheduling in the library media center. Also, resources beyond the school library media center should be available either through online databases or within the community, as students will frequently need more in-depth material than is usually available within the school.

Further, both the classroom teacher and the library media specialist must model the steps in the research process for the students. An explanation of how the credibility and authority of the sources of information was determined is needed. Thinking out loud shows students the thought process when determining what types of questions might be asked. Another example of when to think out loud would be when weighing the value of using surveys, interviews, or experiments in the research. Modeling the steps in the research process for students is a powerful learning tool.

Farmer (2001) discussed how one school changed its approach to teaching information literacy skills. The faculty noticed students were having problems accessing and evaluating information and that incidences of plagiarism were rising. Student research questions were vague and underdeveloped. The school formed a study group co-chaired by the library media specialist and a science teacher, with representatives from all departments. The group identified these research questions: 1) What information skills do students need to demonstrate? and 2) What interventions will improve student skills?

After reviewing research on information literacy, the study group developed a Research Skills Inventory List, which included some skills high school students could be expected to have, such as use of various resources, use of indexes, and note taking. Based on this list, they assessed the students' level of information literacy, thus creating a baseline to use for comparison. They identified some specific areas of need, such as using graphic organizers, comparing different sources on the same topic, and avoiding plagiarism. This process led to the next question about why the gaps in literacy existed. The study group then looked at instructional experiences. Teachers and students independently determined which class required which information literacy skills. The data were then examined to find the gaps, and possible interventions were brainstormed.

The end result was a multi-faceted solution. Research products were developed to standardize bibliographic entries, provide research process and product rubrics, provide a research handbook, and develop a library research Web page. In addition to developing products, inservices were provided for the faculty. One inservice involved having the faculty review where information literacy skills were being taught and negotiating any changes that were needed. Another inservice dealt with evaluating Web sites and how to develop assignments that would make plagiarism difficult.

Faculty involvement is essential for any permanent and meaningful change to take place. Farmer (2001) states that this approach to solving a problem worked well because it grew out of a teacher-perceived need, the effort was student centered, classroom teachers partnered with the library media specialist and took leadership roles where needed; and the entire faculty being involved gave them ownership of the process and results.

Advantages

The advantages of problem-based, inquiry-based, resource-based, or project-based instruction are similar. Students are more highly motivated to learn because the instruction is centered on a problem of interest to them. This is the motivating factor the brain needs to stimulate learning. Problems about which students must draw their own conclusions through asking why, how, and which are best because they give the student time to practice and develop the needed neural networks that result in learning. By creating problems that require thinking, plagiarism is more easily avoided.

Issues in Implementation

Even if there is agreement that project-based, inquiry-based, problem-based, or resource-based learning are the best ways to develop information literacy skills and life-long learning and help students meet standards, there are obstacles that must be overcome, including lack of time, scheduling, confusion of roles, lack of professional development and training, and poorly defined assignments.

More and more teachers are feeling the lack of time to teach what they feel students should know. State standards require that certain skills be taught and assessments completed. Add local requirements, and teachers feel overwhelmed by having to complete all requirements. As one teacher said, "There is no time to teach the fun things, the things kids enjoy" (Susan Braun, personal conversation, April 23, 2002). No wonder teachers are reluctant to undertake anything new or consider a new way of doing something. One of the key points to be made is that project-based, inquiry-based, problem-based, and resource-based learning are not methods to be tacked on to the fun activities. They are legitimate teaching methods that can be used to teach not only the information literacy skills but other content as well. Giving lectures and handing out worksheets before using one of the above methods is not a requirement. Substituting one of these methods when appropriate will add enthusiasm and fun for the students.

Following is an example of how one media specialist took a classroom objective and information literacy objectives and designed a learning experience for second graders.

> Classroom Objective: The student will understand what is involved in various occupations and decide if their "job" will be a service to people or a job that produces goods for people.
>
> Information Literacy Objectives: The student will 1) become familiar with the Super 3 research process; 2) learn to take notes; and 3) use Kidspiration? to create a final product.
>
> Learning Activity: The teacher made two templates in Kidspiration and put them in each student's class folder on the computer server. One template was for taking notes and the second was a graphic organizer to enter the information they found. Students worked with a partner to do the research, but each took notes and put the information in templates.
>
> Students then shared their information orally with the class by using the graphic organizers.
>
> Evaluation: Students were to think back on their projects and deciding what they did that was good, what did they like about the project, and how they could have done better. (Sherry Bishop, personal communication, 2004)

Scheduling in schools is horrific. Teachers complain about having the entire class for only two hours a day because students are taken from the classroom for special classes, speech therapy, and other activities. Some elementary schools have a block of time for reading and language arts that is almost sacred. Not surprisingly, teachers groan when the library media specialist wants to talk about information literacy skills. The key to success is for the library media specialist to show the teacher how the subject matter objectives can be taught at the same time that the information literacy objectives are taught. Curriculum mapping can be used as a way to target units and topics where information literacy skills can be taught. (See chapter 4 for further discussion of curriculum mapping.)

When teachers do work with library media specialists on teaching information literacy skills, there is often confusion about who is doing what. Teachers need to understand that their role is providing the curriculum objectives and the assignment. The library media specialist provides a process and resources. Together they must reach a consensus about what will be taught and how and by whom. Ideally, team teaching occurs. Even if the library media specialist is teaching the objective, the classroom teacher should be present. Not only does the teacher know what students are learning, but he or she can also provide valuable connections to previous learning.

The library media specialist can help clear up this confusion by learning to diagnose the teacher's information needs. Grover and Carabell (1995) suggested these steps in a diagnostic process:

- Establish a comfortable relationship with the teacher. Use positive, nonverbal communication, show interest in the teacher, and create an engaging physical environment.

- Determine the context for the information need. Determine where the teacher is in the search process, what the purpose of using the information is, and the expected outcomes.

- Determine the information preferences of the teacher. Identify preferred formats for researching and for reporting information and special requirements.

- Ascertain the teacher's limitations. Constraints of time, cost, and availability are top on the list of limitations teachers feel.

- Evaluate the appropriateness of the information. Elicit feedback on the teacher's comfort, appropriateness of information to the context, preferences, and limitations.

In the process of diagnosing the information needs, the library media specialist can often clarify what needs to be done by the teacher in order for the collaboration to be successful.

Clearly defined assignments are a must. No longer is it acceptable to assign students to "look up something about a sea animal." By engaging in problem-based learning, students can see the relevance of what they are asked to learn. They can also better design research strategies to solve the problem. There must be guidelines about what students are expected to know (the curriculum). They need to know how to go about finding the information (the process). They need access to appropriate resources. Assignments and the research process must be designed to meet the learning stage of students. Students should be expected to ask questions to help them determine the information they need. Even kindergartners can begin to define what they want to know if they are asked, for example, to state what they want to know about a whale.

If a focus on problem solving and information process is to become a reality, certain aspects of thinking about teaching and how students learn must change. Changing how teachers think about teaching and learning comes about through working together to examine why change is needed, how student learning will improve, and how to implement the change. Change will not happen overnight. More than likely, it will take years. Not all teachers or library media specialists will make the change at the same time. There will be those who jump on the bandwagon immediately. Others will change only as they see the benefits. Others wait to make sure this is not just a fad. Sadly, some never make the change.

Sufficient time, clearly defined roles, and well-constructed assignments help ensure the success of inquiry-based learning. With a commitment to inquiry-based learning, mutually held constructive beliefs, and collaboration between classroom teachers and the library media specialists, students will succeed in becoming effective and efficient information users, meeting the information literacy standards. Research on how people learn shows that using a process must be repeated frequently and in a variety of situations. In other words, students need to experience problem-solving assignments and the research process every year and in all curricula.

Conclusion

As stated in *Information Power: Building Partnerships For Learning*, "The goal (of information literacy) is to assist all students in becoming active and creative locators, evaluators, and users of information to solve problems and to satisfy their own curiosity" (AASL & AECT, 1998, p. 2). One method is not better than the other in achieving this goal. The library media specialist and teacher must decide which is best for a given objective. Direct instruction by teachers is still appropriate in some instances. The teacher and library media specialist must decide the best approach to use with students. Keep in mind that the learning is still structured, but the student rather than the teacher has moved to the center of the stage. The emphasis is on learning rather than instructing.

Central to any of the methods is a research question that requires problem solving or decision making, "real-world problems." Unlimited access to a collection of materials is essential. Students must develop the skills to take information from different formats and blend that learning into new knowledge. For learning to truly be long term, interdisciplinary learning and connections between school and community must be made. Because some new learning takes longer than others, projects could take a few days or all year.

Students benefit from using any of the methods of instruction discussed above. All require students to work collaboratively at some point. At the same time, the learning can be structured so that individuals who prefer to work alone can do so, at least part of the time. There is greater flexibility in meeting individual learning styles. The learning can be structured to work with any age group from primary through higher education. All the methods promote critical thinking and using a research process.

Regardless of the method of instruction—resource-based, project-based, inquiry-based, or problem-based—the teacher and library media specialist take on a new role, guiding students through a research process and developing critical thinking skills. Teachers and library media specialists assume the role of guide rather than dispenser of knowledge. Students assume more responsibility for their own learning. The result will be students who learn to be critical thinkers and have a process for problem solving they can use the rest of their lives.

CHAPTER 9

How Did I Do?: Assessment

Questions students frequently ask are, "Is this okay?" or "How did I do?" We all want to know how we did. Assessment is a part of the learning process. From our mistakes we learn how to improve. Stripling reminds us that student learning must be measured in terms of ability to "do" as well as to "know" (1999). Standardized tests often measure only what students know. Local school districts must measure students' ability to do a task. *Assessment* in this chapter refers to evaluation of the information literacy skills and the research process.

If library media specialists believe that critical thinking and being able to use a research process are important and critical life skills, the assessment of what students know must go beyond the knowledge level. Students must be expected to demonstrate synthesis and application as defined by Bloom's taxonomy. Wiggins and McTighe (2001) state that understanding is always a matter of degree. In *Understanding by Design* they discuss six facets of understanding—explanation, interpretation, application, perspective, empathizing, and self-knowledge—and how each might be assessed:

> Explanation is thorough, supported and justifiable accounts of phenomena, facts, and data. Assessments can be performance tasks, projects, prompts, and tests that ask students to explain and link specific fact to larger ideas and justify connections. Students go beyond just giving the answer to show their work and explain their answer.
>
> Interpretation is telling meaningful stories, offering apt translations, or providing a historical or personal dimension to ideas or events. To demonstrate this type of understanding students must be able to read, view, or listen and interpret what they read, saw, or heard.
>
> Application is effectively using and adapting what is known in many different contexts. Assessment of application calls authentic tasks or application to real world situations. Conventional tests can be used to supplement the assessment.

Perspective is seeing and hearing points of view through
critical eyes and ears. Essential questions are critical to helping
students see different points of view as well as to aiding in the assessment of the student learning.

Empathiz[ing] is finding value in what others might find un-
usual or perceiving sensitively on the basis of prior direct experience. Assessment of empathy centers on whether or not students
have overcome egocentrism, ethnocentrism, and present-cen-
teredness regardless of the actual method used to assess the
learning.

Self-knowledge perceives the personal style, prejudices,
projections and habits of mind that shape and impede our own
understanding. In other words, we know what we don't know
and why. Here is where self-assessment fits. Students need to be
taught how to evaluate their own learning realistically.

Wiggins and McTighe (2001) argue that the assessment should be determined first. What is it that students should know as a result of instruction? Local and state standards should be consulted at this point. Then determine what
is acceptable evidence that learning has taken place. Any benchmarks or indicators that are used with the standards might be helpful. Last, determine the
learning experiences and instructional activities. The point at which what is
acceptable evidence is determined is when the method of assessment becomes relevant.

Wiggins and McTighe (2001) further contend that assessment is a matter
of what is more or less naïve or sophisticated; more or less superficial or
in-depth. What the teacher and library media specialist are looking for in assessment is what degree of understanding the student has reached. This assessment commonly takes place at the end of a project, but assessments may
well take place periodically during a project. Working together, the classroom teacher and the library media specialist must determine what the characteristics or indicators of learning along a continuum are, from just beginning
to learn to advanced learner.

Just how does the library media specialist go about assessing what students have learned? How can the teacher find out the students' degree of understanding? There are many different methods of assessment, including
written tests of various types, portfolios, products or projects, rubrics, and
performances. No one method is best in all instances. The library media specialist and the classroom teacher will determine which method of assessment to use based on what the students should know at the end of the

learning experience. A decision will also be made about who will do the assessing. Sometimes the assessment will be done by the teacher, other times by the library media specialist, and at times by both.

Authentic Assessments

While students should know the content of a subject, they should also be able to use that knowledge in an authentic or real-world situation. In an interview Howard Gardner stated that there is a need to develop assessments that are much more representative of what human beings are going to have to do to survive in this society (cited in Checkley, 1997, p. 12). An authentic assessment requires a connection to the "real world" or a simulation of the real world, in other words, an application of what has been learned (Bergen, 1994). Assessment of understanding should be grounded in authentic performances (Wiggins & McTighe, 2001). Counting the number of resources used or the number of note cards written is no longer acceptable. Assessment needs, for example, to focus more on the appropriateness of the resources. Authentic assessment values both the processes and products involved in learning (Callison & Lamb, 2004). Students need feedback on how well they completed the steps of the research process as well as the outcome of what they learned.

The National Science Education Standards define authentic assessments as ones "that require students to perform complex tasks representative of activities actually done in out-of-school settings" (*Classroom assessment,* 2001, p. 31). Since out-of-school settings are not always possible, simulations are often used. One of the main differences between the traditional paper-and-pencil assessments (true/false, fill-in-the blank, and multiple-choice) and authentic assessment is that paper-and-pencil tests are usually given after learning has taken place. Authentic assessments are used as a part of the learning experience and can take place periodically throughout a project. The process of learning becomes as important as the content. Authentic assessment also allows some freedom in developing the final product or project in such a way as to meet individual learning styles, which is not always possible with multiple-choice tests.

Some types of assessments are discussed below. In authentic assessment, providing feedback for student improvement is as important as evaluating student work. Also, the focus of authentic assessment is on individual strengths and weaknesses rather than comparing students (Callison & Lamb, 2004). Whatever type of assessment is used, when designing the assessment tool a good practice is to have it reviewed by a peer to ensure that what is being assessed is what is actually meant to be assessed and that the scoring criteria are clear.

Performance Assessments

Assessment by using performances is useful in those instances where paper-and-pencil tests and portfolios are not suitable. Performance assessment requires students to demonstrate what they know and what they can do. These assessments allow students to demonstrate their understanding and skills as they perform certain activities. Students are evaluated on their ability to perform specific tasks and the products created in the process (*Classroom assessment,* 2001). A performance might be, for example, an oral presentation, an enactment, a debate, or a dramatic reading.

According to Bergen (1994), a performance assessment has three qualities:

- Its many facets are measured simultaneously.

- It is applied, having the complexity of real-world roles.

- It may be individual, but if it is group based the performance of every member is evaluated as well as the group's.

To be successful performance assessment must have defined, explicit standards of performance and provide multiple ways in which children can reach those standards.

Products

A product is something that students create to demonstrate their understanding of certain concepts and skills and/or their ability to apply, analyze, synthesize, or evaluate those concepts and skills (Mueller, 2003). Examples of products are a demonstration, a videotape, a PowerPoint presentation, an exhibit, a research paper, and a poem. Products are usually developed over a period of time and reflect more depth of knowledge and understanding. A rubric is frequently used to assess the learning that has occurred while developing the product. Additional rubrics are used to access the process of learning (the research process) and the product itself.

Benchmarks

A benchmark is a standard against which student learning can be measured. Setting benchmarks is a guide for students as well as an assessment tool for learning. Benchmarks help students understand what the important concepts are and what will be evaluated. By using benchmarks students have some questions to guide their decision making. For example, in evaluating the research process the Iowa City Community School District uses seven basic evaluation skills for sources of information:

1. Appropriateness of sources

2. Availability of sources

3. Relevance of sources

4. Suitability of relevant sources

5. Currency of resources

6. Authority of author or source

7. Reliability of source

With each evaluation skill there are questions to guide students (Iowa City Community School District, 1998):

1. Appropriateness
   a. Do I need general information? Is an encyclopedia or magazine a better choice?
   b. Do I need current information? Is a magazine, book, or Internet a better choice?
   c. Do I need a map? Is a CD-ROM encyclopedia or atlas better?

2. Availability
   a. Can I get the resource on time?
   b. Will there be enough information?
   c. Would time be better spent using a local readily available source?

3. Relevant
   a. Does the table of contents show information on the topic?
   b. Does the index contain a number of pages on the topic?
   c. Does the abstract of the article deal with my topic?

4. Suitability
   a. Can I read and understand it?
   b. Do I understand the title?
   c. If I read a page, are there several words I don't understand?
   d. Can I paraphrase what I just read?

5. Currency
   a. When was the book published?
   b. Does copyright date matter?

6. Authority
   a. Was the person's background or training in the subject?
   b. Has my teacher ever heard of this person?
   c. Is the person clearly identified from what's on the Web page?

7. Reliability
   a. Is it free of stereotypes or loaded words?
   b. Is it a commercial site, personal, or sponsored by an organization?
   c. Are other sources given to support or verify the information?

In order to assess students' understanding of the research process, the library media specialist or teacher could conference with the students about their choice of resources. Another way would be to have students keep Learning Logs (see p. 132) and then review these. A checklist or a rubric might be developed. Figure 9.1 shows how the Iowa City Community School District's seven evaluation skills for sources of information could be turned into a checklist. The statements could be either checked off or answered yes or no. The checklist could become a part of the overall assessment piece.

The benchmarks could be turned into a different checklist and used to keep students on track. Using the benchmarks in a checklists allows students to take responsibility for their own learning through peer and self-evaluation. The benchmarks could also be used to design rubrics for evaluation.

Rubrics

Rubrics are a common way of assessing student work. They can improve student performance by making teacher expectations clear and showing students how to meet those expectations. Grover, Lakin, and Dickerson (1997) define rubrics as guidelines for evaluation using quantitative descriptions or measures for student progress. Goodrich (1997) refers to rubrics as a scoring tool that lists the criteria for a piece of work and articulates gradations of quality for each criterion. Wiggins (reported in Phillip, 2002) describes rubrics as specifying the elements of performance that matter most and detailing how to distinguish strong performances from weak ones.

Sources of Information Checklist

Directions: For each of the sources of information you use make a check mark to indicate the information meets the criteria. A blank space will show the source of information lacks that particular criteria. If the criterion is not appropriate write in NA for not applicable.

Skill	Source 1	Source 2	Source 3
Appropriateness:			
General information			
Current information			
Map available			
Availability:			
Can get on time			
Enough information			
Local resource readily available			
Relevant:			
Table of contents show information			
Index contains several pages on topic			
Abstract deals with topic			
Suitability:			
I can read and understand			
I understand title			
Several words I don't understand			
I can paraphrase what I read			
Currency:			
When published			
Copyright date matters			
Authority:			
Author had training in area			
Teacher familiar with author			
Author clearly identified			
Reliability			
Free of stereotypes or loaded words			
Commercial, personal, or organization sponsored site			
Sources given to support or verify information			

Figure 9.1. Sources of Information Checklist. (Based on Information Literacy Skills of the Iowa City (IA) Community Schools.)

Rubrics can be instructional or evaluative. In fact, the same rubric can serve both purposes. An instructional rubric guides students in what is to be done, and they know the criteria against which they will be judged. The same rubric can then be used as a peer or self-evaluation tool to help students see how they might improve. After giving students an opportunity to make revisions in the product, the teacher or library media specialist can then use the rubric to evaluate that product. Thus the rubric is used in assessment for informative feedback about the work in progress as well as a detailed evaluation of the final product. Andrade (2002) describes an advantage of using rubrics: instructional rubrics provide students with more informative feedback about their strengths and areas in need of improvement than do traditional forms of assessment.

The value of using rubrics with students is that expectations are clearly defined. Using Wiggins and McTighe's (2001) backward design theory, rubrics should be created before the project, followed by the design of the unit and lessons. Rubrics can vary, but they have two characteristics in common: 1) a list of criteria to show what is important in a project or process; and 2) different levels of quality, usually described in terms of good, average, or unacceptable work. The qualities, or gradations as Andrade (2002) calls them, can be written to describe problems that students commonly encounter. By doing this the library media specialist assists the student in understanding what his or her strengths and weaknesses are. Rubrics can also be used to identify goals for improvement.

In the Colony Rubric (see Figure 9.2), the criteria listed are webbing, Venn diagram, and paragraph. The information literacy skill for this lesson is focusing on note taking by using a web. Students were familiar with using Venn diagrams to compare and contrast, so the decision was made to have them make one to guide their thinking in determining which colony they might like to live in. The teacher wanted the students to write a paragraph to explain their reasoning. The levels of quality were explained by using the descriptive words *Exceeds Expectations, Meets Expectations, Near Expectations,* and *Needs Improvement.* These terms are similar to those the school district uses. Since a problem in note taking is students copying sentences, one criterion became that no sentences were copied. The teacher wanted at least three reasons with supporting detail for where a student chose to live, so that had to be included (Brenda Cuba and Joie Taylor, personal experience, 2004).

Category	Exceeds Expectations	Meets Expectations	Near Expectations	Needs Improvement
Webbing Notes	Information pertinent to questions. No sentences; used own words More than 3 points under each topic Readable No misspelled words	Information pertinent to questions. No sentences; used own words 3 points under each topic Readable Few misspelled word	Some information not pertinent to questions Had 1 or 2 points under some topics Used some sentences; some copying Several misspelled words Parts difficult to read	Information incomplete No points under some topics Used some sentences; copied from source Many misspelled words Parts so close difficult to read
Venn Diagram	Had similar information on a New England, Middle, and Southern colony Had numerous points included in all parts of diagram Was able to compare and contrast the colonies and make a decision	Had similar information on a New England, Middle, and Southern colony Had several points included in most parts of diagram Was able to compare and contrast the colonies and make a decision	Lacked information on one colony or some on all of them Could make some comparisons, but a decision was difficult because of lack of information	Did not have information on one of the colonies or was lacking a lot of information. Could not compare and contrast the colonies and make a decision from the information
Paragraph	Stated my choice of colony Had more than 3 supporting reasons with explanations of why those were important Had complete sentences No punctuation or spelling errors	Stated my choice of colony Had 3 supporting reasons with explanations of why those were important Had complete sentences Minor punctuation or spelling errors	Stated my choice of colony. Stated why the choice was made but could not fully explain why. Several misspelled words or incorrect punctuation	Stated my choice of colony Did not explain choice or included the reasons but did not explain why Many misspelled words or incorrect punctuation

Figure 9.2. Colony Rubric.

There is no one way to go about developing a rubric, but there are some key components in all rubrics:

- Identify the desired outcome. What should students be able to do at the end of instruction?

- Determine what student performance would demonstrate achievement of the outcome. What is the best way for students to show what they have learned?

- Establish the criteria to be used for assessment. What will actually be assessed?

- Determine the levels of quality to be met. What is acceptable work, exceptional work, and unacceptable work? How many levels will there be?

- State the levels in performance behaviors.

The criteria to be used in a rubric are listed in a column on the left. Rubrics can have several levels of quality, which are listed in columns to the right of the criteria. Grover, Larkin, and Dickerson (1997) used four levels of achievement—Application, Demonstration, Understanding, and Awareness—with Application being the highest level and Awareness the lowest. They also included "not applicable or no evidence is available." In developing their levels of achievement, the Iowa City Community School District (1998) chose to use Expert, Proficient, Apprentice, and Novice. Some library media specialists choose to use a numerical or point system. Although rubrics were never meant to be tied to grades, some schools do just that by using a numerical system of 0 to 4, with 0 being a failing grade and 4 an A. Schools often have defined standard levels of quality to be used throughout the district, and the library media specialist would be expected to follow those.

One of the problems with rubrics is the language used in describing the levels of achievement. Words such as *most, often, poor,* and *excellent* are difficult to describe objectively. Some library media specialists solve the problem by saying, "Students should have three resources," but that takes us back to counting the number of resources used. For this reason the practice of having someone else use the rubric and give feedback about clarification and ease of use is a good idea.

If rubrics are to accomplish the task of improving student performance, the rubric must be shared with students at the beginning of instruction. Students can use a rubric to guide their work. When students know what is expected of them, the library media specialist or teacher can easily hold them accountable for the work. Handing students a rubric is not enough. Initially the teacher or library media specialist should check with students throughout a project to see how they are doing in using the rubric as a guide to accomplishing their work. After students have used several rubrics and are comfortable with them, the library media specialist might have the students help design the rubric to be used for a specific unit or lesson.

The library media specialist need not always begin from scratch when developing rubrics. Several Internet sites provide helpful templates and suggestions by subject area. Rubistar, located at http://rubistar.4teachers.org, is one example.

Portfolios

Callison (1993) defines portfolios as a deliberate compilation, gathered according to a plan, for use by a specified reader for a specified purpose. Another way of describing a portfolio is "a purposeful and representative collection of student work that conveys a story of progress, achievement and/or effort. The student is involved in selecting pieces of work and includes self-reflections of what understandings the piece of work demonstrates. Thus, criteria for selection and evaluation need to be made clear prior to selection" (*Classroom assessment,* 2001, p. 31). What is included in a portfolio depends on its purpose. Is the purpose to show growth over a period of time? If so, work from the beginning, at several points along the way, and at the end should be included. Portfolios might be designed to demonstrate the learning process. In this instance work that shows development of a skill or a process used would be included. Is the portfolio the final product or best work of the student? In this case the items included would be those that demonstrate what has been learned or show the best work.

The teacher and the library media specialist will determine together the purpose of the portfolio and what evidence the student should present. The Harvard Graduate School of Education suggests the following elements for a portfolio:

- A collection of student work that demonstrates what has been learned and understood

- An extended time frame to allow progress and effort to be demonstrated

- Structure and organizing principles to help organize and interpret and analyze

- Student involvement in selection of materials for portfolio and in reflection and assessment (reported in *Classroom assessment,* 2001, p.62).

The types of items that might be put into a portfolio are many: essays, research papers, CD-ROMs, PowerPoint presentations, a videotape of presentations, drawings, etc. The list is practically infinite. The focus has to be on why the portfolio is being developed. A portfolio to help students develop research process skills might include the following:

- Brainstorming concerning the task or critical question

- What resources were considered and the thought process to determine which would be used

- A time line showing progress on the work

- A learning log of successes and difficulties

- Actual notes that were taken

- Feedback along the way from the library media specialist

- Drafts of the final project

- The finished project or a CD-ROM or videotape if actual project, such as an oral presentation, cannot be included

- Student reflection on the overall project

If the portfolio is to be shared with parents or others not familiar with the classroom experience, a table of contents or cover letter written by the student should be included.

Learning Logs

Observations, conferencing, and interviews allow students and teachers to explore together a student's achievement and discuss strengths and weaknesses. Learning logs are useful in helping facilitate a dialog between students and the library media specialist or teacher. Stripling (1993) advocates the use of learning logs as a way to assess student thinking, specifically in the note-taking process. Students set up two columns in a notebook, one for notes and the other for reactions to the notes. The reactions can include personal reactions, feelings, or questions to be pursued further. Helping students learn to interact mentally and emotionally with their notes is the purpose of a learning log. Learning logs document students' involvement in their own learning process and are consistent with Wiggins and McTighe's work on developing understanding. Learning logs also help facilitate a dialog between a student and the library media specialist. The library media specialist can ask questions or make suggestions to assist the student in the research process. Personal contacts are often useful when students are working on group projects, as this is an avenue to work out problems within the group such as one person dominating it or someone not working.

Other Assessments

Tests

Paper-and-pencil tests are still valid, but to evaluate both the content learned and the process, testing must go beyond true/false, fill-in-the blank, and multiple-choice questions. Although these might give the classroom teacher an idea of how well the content has been learned, there is no evidence of understanding the process. Wiggins (2000) argues that for tests to be valid they must meet two criteria: 1) comprehensive evidence of the factual knowledge and 2) comprehensive evidence of student work showing or explaining the strategies used to answer the questions.

There are different ways of showing evidence of factual knowledge, such as pre- and post-tests; tests that assess factual information, concepts, and skills that were taught; end-of-course tests; norm-referenced or criterion-referenced tests; and skills checklists. Comprehensive evidence of student work usually involves problem solving, critical thinking, and writing. Multiple-step questions in which students have to explain their thinking might be used.

Simple Assessments

Nonverbal means of evaluating should be used with young students. Smiley faces are commonly used (see Figure 9.3, p. 134). A quick evaluation of the process can be done by giving students the sheet, reading it to them, and having them mark the appropriate face.

A thumb's-up or thumb's-down is another quick way to see if students have learned a concept. One library media specialist taught kindergarten students the sign language letters for the A, T, and I. She also taught that A stood for the word *author,* T for the word *title,* and I for the word *illustrator.* When she asked students, for example, "Who wrote the words in the book?" the students would make the sign for the letter A. She could then quickly see who knew the word and who did not.

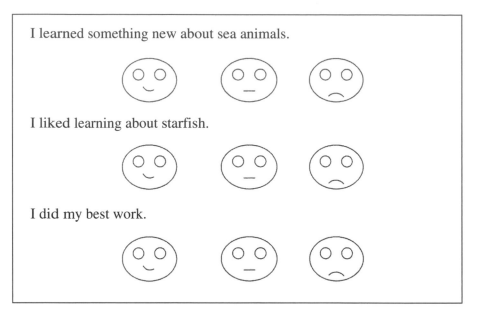

Figure 9.3. Evaluation Tool for Primary Students.

Conclusion

Assessment is a vital part of student learning. The key to successful assessment is knowing what is important. What is it that students should know as a result of instruction? The second key is to know what is acceptable as evidence that learning has taken place. Paper-and-pencil tests still have a place in assessment, especially in determining the content knowledge. However, teachers and library media specialists cannot rely on knowledge alone to ensure that students can actually use what they have learned. Today assessment must include whether or not students understand the process or can transfer what they know to a different situation.

Students must also understand the role of assessment in education. Knowing by what criteria they will be assessed empowers students to take control of their learning. They understand both the aim of their work and what it means to complete it successfully. In order to complete their work successfully students need to be able to assess their own progress toward meeting the goals or objectives the teacher has set. Only through learning these skills and taking responsibility for their own accomplishments will students become independent learners. The role of the library media specialist and the classroom teacher, working together, is to determine which of the many methods of assessment to use, and who will do the assessment, including any student self-assessment.

References

Aha! Of media literacy, The. (1999). *Education Update, 41* (7), 1, 6–7.

Allen, C. (Ed). (1999). *Skills for life: Information literacy for grades K–6* (2d ed.). Worthington, OH: Linworth Publishing.

American Association of School Librarians and the Association for Educational Communications and Technology (AASL & AECT). (1988). *Information power: Guidelines for school library media programs.* Chicago: American Library Association.

American Association of School Librarians and the Association for Educational Communications and Technology (AASL & AECT). (1998). *Information power: Building partnerships for learning.* Chicago: American Library Association.

American Library Association. (1989). *Presidential Committee on Information Literacy: Final report.* [Online]. Available: http://www.ala.org/acrl/acrlpubs/whitepapers/presidential.htm (accessed March 2005).

Anderson, M. A. (1999). Creating the link: Aligning national and state standards. *Book Report, 17* (5), 12–14.

Andrade, H. G. (2002). Using rubrics to promote thinking and learning. *Educational Leadership, 57* (5), 13–19.

Association for Supervision and Curriculum Development (ASCD). (1995). Developing information literacy: Advocates promote resource-based learning. *Education Update, 37* (2), 1.

Association of College & Research Libraries. (2001). *Presidential Committee on Information Literacy.* Chicago: American Library Association.

Barron, D. D. (2003). Ideas and information for the library media specialist's new year. *School Library Media Activities Monthly, 20* (1), 49–51.

Bergen, D. (1994). Authentic performance assessments. *Childhood Education, 70* (2), 99–102.

Black, P., Harrison, C., Lee, C., Marshall, B., & William, D. (2004) Working inside the black box: assessment for learning in the classroom. *Phi Delta Kappan, 86* (1), 9–22.

Bransford, J. D. (Ed.). (2000). *How people learn: Brain, mind, experiences and school.* Washington, DC: National Academy Press.

Buck Institute for Education. (2002). *Project based learning handbook.* [Online]. Available: http://bie.org/pbl/pblhandbook/intro.php (accessed February 14, 2005).

Buzzeo, T. (2002) Collaboration: Working with restrictions. *Library Talk, 15* (2), 26–27.

California School Library Association. (1997). *From library skills to information literacy: A handbook for the 21st century.* (2d ed.). San Jose, CA: Hi Willow Research and Publishing.

Callison, D. (1993). The potential for portfolio assessment. *School Library Media Annual, 11,* 30–39.

Callison, D. (2003a).Learning resources, part II. *School Library Media Activities Monthly, 19* (10), 31–35.

Callison, D. (2003b). Information Fluency. *School Library Media Activities Monthly, 20* (4), 38–39.

Callison, D., & Lamb, A. (2004). Authentic learning. *School Library Media Activities Monthly, 21* (4), 34–39.

Carroll, F. L. (1981). *Recent advances in school librarianship.* Oxford: Pergamon Press.

Checkley, K. (1997). The first seven . . . and the eight: A conversation with Howard Gardner. *Educational Leadership, 55* (1), 8–13.

Classroom assessment and the National Science Education Standards. (2001). Washington, D.C., National Academy Press.

Colorado Department of Education. (2002). *Colorado information literacy.* [Online]. Available: http://www.cde.state.co.us/cdelib/slinfolitindex.htm (accessed July 16, 2004).

Columbus Public Schools. (1998). *Information literacy K–12 Curriculum Guide.* Columbus, NE: Author.

CTAP information literacy guidelines K–12. (2001). [Online]. Available: http://ctap.fcoe.k12.ca.us/ctap/Info.Lit/Guidelines.html (accessed June 4, 2001).

Doiron, R., & Davis, J. (1998). *Partners in learning: Students, teachers, and the school library.* Englewood, CO: Libraries Unlimited.

Donham, J. (1999). Collaboration in the media center: Building partnerships for learning. *NASSP Bulletin, 83* (605), 20–26.

Donham, J., Bishop, K., Kuhlthau, C. C., & Oberg, D. (2001). *Inquiry-based learning: Lessons from Library Power.* Worthington, OH: Linworth Publishing.

Doyle, C. S. (1994). *Information literacy in an information society: A concept for the information age.* Syracuse, NY: Eric Clearinghouse on Information & Technology. ED372763.

Eisenberg, M. B., & Berkowitz, R. E. (1988). *Curriculum initiative: An agenda and strategy for library media programs.* Norwood, NJ: Ablex Publishing Corp.

Eisenberg, M. B., & Berkowitz, R. E. (1999). *Teaching information & technology skills: The Big6 in elementary schools.* Worthington, OH: Linworth Publishing.

Eisenburg, M. B., Carrie, A., & Spitzer, K. L. (2004). *Information literacy: Essential skills for the information age* (2d ed.). Westport, CT: Libraries Unlimited.

Extra Edge, The. (1995). *A lever and a fulcrum: How school media center specialists can become powerful change agents for their schools.* Satellite teleconference, April 27.

Facione, P. A. (1998). *Critical thinking: What it is and why it counts.* [Online]. Available: http://www.calpress.com/pdf_files/what& why.pdf (accessed January 8, 2005).

Farmer, L. (1999). Making information literacy a schoolwide reform effort. *The Book Report, 18* (3), 6–8.

Farmer, L. (2001). *Information literacy: A whole school reform approach.* Presented at the Judith Pitts Research Form, American Association of School Librarians Conference. Indianapolis, IN.

Findings from the evaluation of the national Library Power Program. (1999). New York: DeWitt Wallace-Reader's Digest Fund.

Goodrich, H. (1997). Understanding rubrics. *Educational Leadership, 54* (4), 14–17.

Grover, R. & Carabell, J. (1995). Diagnosing information needs in a school library media center. *School Library Media Activities Monthly, 11* (5), 32–36, 48.

Grover, R., Lakin, McMahon, J., & Dickerson, J. (1997). *An interdisciplinary model for assessing learning.* Syracuse, NY: Eric Clearinghouse. ED4125948.

Harada, V., & Kim, L. (2003). *Problem based instruction: Making learning real.* Conference presentation at the American Association of Librarians conference. Kansas City, MO, October 23–25.

Harbour, D. (2002). Collection mapping. *The Book Report, 20* (5), 6–10.

Hardiman, M. M. (2003). *Connecting brain research with effective teaching: The brain-targeted teaching model.* Lanham, MD: Scarecrow Press.

Hartzell, G. N. (1994). *Building influence for the school librarian.* Worthington, OH: Linworth Publishing.

Haycock, K. (1996). The impact of scheduling on cooperative programming and teaching and information skills instruction. In *School libraries: research findings: Research on flexible access to school libraries.* [Online]. Available: http://www.nswtl.net/info/research/flexible.htm (accessed November 28, 2003).

Haycock, K. (1999). *Collaborative programme planning and teaching.* [Online]. Available: http://www.teacherlibrarian.com/what_works_V.27.html (accessed March 5, 2005).

Herrin, B. (1994). Collaboration: Leadership style of the 90s. *Library Power.* (January/February), 4, 5.

Horace. (1995). Providence, RI: The Coalition of Essential Schools.

Hughes-Hassell, S., & Wheelock, A. (Eds.) (2001). *The Information powered school.* Chicago: American Library Association.

Introduction to inquiry-based learning, An. (2001). [Online]. Available: http://www.youthlearn.org/ learning/approach/inquiry.asp (accessed January 9, 2005).

Iowa City Community School District. (1998). *Developing an information literacy program K–12: A How-to-do-it manual and CD-ROM package.* New York: Neal-Schuman Publishers.

Jacobs, H. H. (1997). *Mapping the big pictures: Integrating curriculum and assessment K–12.* Alexandria, VA: Association for Supervision and Curriculum Development.

Jay, M. E., & Jay, H. (1990). The principal and the library media program. *School Library Media Activities Monthly, 19* (6), 30–32.

Jones, A. J., Gardner, C., & Zaenglein, J. I. (1998). Desperately seeking standards. *Knowledge Quest, 26* (3), 38–42.

Joyce, M. Z., & Tallman, J. I. (1997). *Making the writing and research connection with the I-Search process.* New York: Neal-Schuman.

Karpisek, M. (1989). *Policymaking for school library media programs.* Chicago: American Library Association.

Katz, L. G. (1995). *Talks with teachers of young children: A collection.* Norwood, NJ: Ablex Publishing.

Kuhlthau, C. C. (1987). An emerging theory of library instruction. *School Library Media Quarterly,* 16(1), 23–27.

Kuhlthau, C. C. (1989). Information search process: A summary of research and implications for school library media programs. *School Library Media Quarterly, 18* (1), 19–25.

Kuhlthau, C. C. (1991). Inside the search process: Information seeking from the user's perspective. *Journal of the American Society for Information Science, 42* (5), 361–371.

Kuhlthau, C. C. (1994a). Information skills for an information society: A review of research. In Christina S. Doyle (Ed.). *Information literacy in an information society: A concept for the information age* (p. 8). Syracuse, NY: Eric Clearinghouse on Information & Technology.

Kuhlthau, C.C. (1994b). *Teaching the library research process.* Metuchen, N.J: Scarecrow Press.

Lance, K. C., & Loertscher, D. (2003). *Power achievement: School library media programs make a difference: The evidence* (2d ed.). Salt Lake City, UT: Hi Willow Research & Publishing.

Lance, K. C., Rodney, M. J., & Hamilton-Pennell, C. (2000). *How school librarians help kids achieve standards: The second Colorado study.* San Jose, CA: Hi Willow Research & Publishing.

Lance, K. C., Welborn, L., & Hamilton-Pennell, C. (1993). *The impact of school library media centers on academic achievement.* Castle Rock, CO: Hi Willow Research & Publishing.

Langford, L. (1998). Information literacy: A clarification. *School Libraries Worldwide, 4* (1), 59–72.

Laverty, C. (1998). *Critical thinking & information use.* [Online]. Available http://stauffer.queensu.ca/inforef/instruct/critical.htm (accessed January 9, 2005).

Laverty, C. (2001). *Resource-based learning.* [Online]. Available: http://stauffer.queensu.ca/ inforef/tutorials/rbl (accessed January 9, 2005).

Lenox, M. F., & Walker, M. L. (1993). Information literacy in the educational process. *The Educational Forum, 57* (3), 312–324.

Leonard, L., & Leonard, P. (2003). *The continuing trouble with collaboration: Teachers talk.* [Online]. Available: http://cie.asu.edu/ volume6/number15. (accessed November 22, 2004).

Library Power project: Executive summary. (2003). In *School libraries: Research findings.* [Online]. Available: http://www.nswtl.net/info/ research/flexible.htm (accessed April 3, 2004).

Lincoln Public Schools Foundation. (2003). *Guide to integrated information literacy skills*. Lincoln, NE: Author.

Loertscher, D. V. (1996). A farewell challenge. *School Library Media Quarterly, 24* (4), 192–194.

Loertscher, D. V. (2002). *Reinventing your school's library in the age of technology: A guide for principals and superintendents* (2d ed.). San Jose, CA: Hi Willow Research & Publishing.

Loertscher, D. V., & Achterman, D. (2002). *Increasing academic achievement through the library media center: A guide for teachers*. San Jose, CA: Hi Willow Research & Publishing.

Logan, D. K. (2000). *Information skills toolkit: Collaborative integrated instruction for the middle grades*. Worthington, OH: Linworth Publishing.

Maryland State Department of Education. (2004). *Questioning for quality thinking*. [Online]. Available: http://www.bcps.org/offices/lis/office/inst/questthinking.html (accessed January 10, 2005).

McGregor, J. H. (1999). *Implementing flexible scheduling in elementary libraries*. ERIC. ED 437 053.

McGregor, J. H. (2003). *The principal and flexible scheduling*. [Online]. Available: http://athene.riv.esu.edu.au/~jmcgrego/ISISlfex.htm (accessed November 11, 2003).

McGriff, N., Harvey, C. A, & Preddy, L. B. (2004). Collecting the data: Collaboration. *School Library Media Activities Monthly, 20* (8), 27–31.

McKenzie, J. A. (2000). *Beyond technology: Questioning, research and the information literate school.* Bellingham, WA: FNO Press.

McKenzie, J. A. (2001). *From trivial pursuit to essential questions and standards-based learning*. [Online]. Available: http://fno.org/feb01/pl.html (accessed January 10, 2005).

McKenzie, J. A. (2002). *Beyond IT*. [Online]. Available: http://optin1server.net/fromnow/Sept00/beyond.html (accessed March 5, 2005).

McKeown, M. G. & Beck, I. L. (1999). Getting the discussion started. *Educational Leadership, 57* (3), 25–28.

Milbury, P. (2005). Collaboration: Ten important reasons to take it seriously. *Knowledge Quest, 33* (5), 30–32.

Monck, D. (1999). Schedules and planning and forms, oh my! *Library Talk, 12* (4), 11.

Moore, P. A., & St. George A. (1991). Children as information seekers: The cognitive demands of books and library systems. *School Library Media Quarterly, 19* (3), 161–168.

Mueller, J. (2003). Authentic tasks. *Authentic assessment toolbox.* [Online]. Available: http://jonathan.mueller.faculty.noctrl.edu/toolbox.tasks.htm (accessed January 10, 2005).

Nebraska Department of Education. (2001). *Academic Standards.* [Online]. Available: http://www.nde.state.ne.us.ndestandards/AcadStand.html (accessed February 11, 2005).

Nebraska Educational Media Association. (1999). *Correlations of the Nebraska L.E.A.R.N.S Standards reading/writing, science, social studies/history and technology with the information literacy standards for student learning.* Lincoln, Neb.: Author.

Oberg, D., Hay, L., & Henri, J. (2000). The role of the principal in an information literate school community: Design and administration of an international research project. *School Library Media Research.* [Online]. Available: http://www.ala.org/ala/aasl/aaslpubsandjournals/slmrb/slmrcontents/volume32000/volume32000.htm (accessed March 5, 2005).

Ohlrich, K. B. (1992). Flexible scheduling: The dream vs. reality. *School Library Journal, 38* (5), 35–38.

Pappas, M. L. (2000). Pathways to inquiry. *School Library Activities Monthly, 16* (9), 23–27.

Partnerships for the 21st Century. (2004). [Online]. Available: http://www.21stcenturyskills.org/ index.php (accessed August 7, 2005).

Perkins, D. (1999). The many faces of constructivism. *Educational Leadership, 57* (3), 6–11.

Phillip, C. (2002). Clear expectations: Rubrics and scoring guides. *Knowledge Quest,* 31(2), 26–27.

Pickard, P. W. (1999). Current research: The instructional consultant role of the school library media specialist. *School Library Media Review.* [Online]. Available: http://www.ala.org/aasl/SLMR/SIMR_resources/select_pickard.html (accessed March 17, 2001).

Pitts, J. (1995) cited in Thomas, N. P. (1999). *Information literacy skills instruction: Applying research to practice in the school library media center.* Englewood, CO: Libraries Unlimited.

Policy Directions. (1998). In Langford, Linda (Ed.). *Information literacy: A clarification.* [Online]. Available: http://fno.org/oct98/clarify.html (accessed June 11, 2003).

Rader, H. B. (1995). In *Understanding information literacy.* [Online]. Available: http://www.ed.gov/pubs/UnderLit/info-literacy.html (accessed June 11, 2003).

Rader, H. B. (1997). Educating students for the information age: The role of the librarian. *Reference Services Review, 25* (2), 47–52.

Rankin, V. (1999). *The thoughtful researcher: Teaching the research process to middle school students.* Englewood, CO: Libraries Unlimited.

School, Children, and Young People's Section of the Nebraska Library Association and the Nebraska Educational Media Association. (2000). *Collaborative planning: Partnerships between teachers and library media specialists.* Lincoln, NE: Author

Schroeder, E. E., & Zarinnia, E. A. (2001) *Problem based learning: Developing information literacy through solving real world problems.* Presentation at the American Association of Librarians Conference. Indianapolis, IN.

Secretary's Commission on Achieving Necessary Skills (SCANS) report. (2000). In Thompson, Helen M., & Henley, Susan A. (Eds.). *Fostering information literacy: Connecting national standards, Goals 2000, and the SCANS report* (p. 21). Englewood, CO: Libraries Unlimited.

Shannon, D. M. (1996). Tracking the transition to a flexible access library program in two Library Power elementary schools. *School Library Media Quarterly, 24* (3), 155–163.

Smilkstein, R. (2003). *We're born to learn.* Thousand Oaks, CA: Corwin Press.

Spitzer, K. (1999). Information literacy: Facing the challenge. *Book Report*, 18(1), 26–28.

Spitzer, K., with Eisenberg, M. B., & Lowe, C. A. (1998). *Information literacy: Essential skills for the information age.* Syracuse, NY: ERIC Clearinghouse on Information & Technology. ED427780.

Stripling, B. (1993). Practicing authentic assessment in the school library. *School Library Media Annual, 11*, 40–57.

Stripling, B. K. (1999). Expectations for achievement and performance: assessing student skills. *NASSP Bulletin, 83* (605), 44–52.

Stripling, B. K., & Pitts, J. M. (1988). *Brainstorms and blueprints: teaching library research as a thinking process.* Englewood, CO: Libraries Unlimited.

Thomas, M. (2002). What is collaboration to you? *Library Talk, 15* (2), 17–18.

Thomas, N. P. (1999). *Information literacy skills instruction: Applying research to practice in the school library media center.* Englewood, CO: Libraries Unlimited.

Thompson, H. M., & Henley, S. A. (2000). *Fostering information literacy: Connecting national standards, Goals 2000, and the SCANS Report.* Englewood, CO: Libraries Unlimited.

Todd, R. J. (1995). Integrated information skills instruction: Does it make a difference? *School Library Media Quarterly, 23* (2), 133–138.

Todd, R. J., & Kuhlthau, C. C. (2004). *Student learning through Ohio school libraries.* Ohio Educational Media Association. [Online]. Available: http://www.oelma.org/studentlearning/default.asp (accessed February 14, 2005).

Tschamler, A. (2002). Top secret: Collaborative efforts really do make a difference. *Library Talk, 15* (2), 14–16.

Understanding University Success. (2003). *Standards for Success.* [Online]. Available: http://www. s4s.org/understanding.php (accessed August 7, 2005).

Van Deusen, J. D., & Tallman, J. I. (1994). The impact of scheduling on curriculum consultation and information skills instruction. *School Library Media Quarterly, 23* (1), 17–25.

Westwater, A., & Wolfe, P. (2000). The brain-compatible curriculum. *Educational Leadership, 58* (3), 49–52.

Wiggins, G. (2000). *Criteria for tests/quizzes.* [Online]. Available: http://www.relearning.org/ resources/PDF/anthol_guide.pdf (accessed January 10, 2005).

Wiggins, G., & McTighe, J. (2001). *Understanding by design.* Upper Saddle River, NJ: Merrill Prentice Hall.

Wisconsin Association of School Librarians. (2000). *Linking Wisconsin's school libraries & classrooms: A guide for integrating information & technology literacy.* Madison: Wisconsin Library Association.

Yucht, A. (1997). *FLIP IT!: An information skills strategy for student researchers.* Worthington, OH: Linworth Publishing.

Yucht, A. (1999). FLIP it! Worksheet formats. *Library Talk, 12* (3), 17–19.

Index

About the Author

JOIE TAYLOR is a school library media specialist from Columbus, Nebraska. She has been active in AASL and other professional associations.